USING THE POWER OF THE WR

BUSINESS COMMUNICATION SKILLS

How to Create High-Impact Letters, Memos, and E-mail

Pat Cramer
& Debra Smith

Dozens of examples to help you write more powerful correspondence

TABLE OF CONTENTS

Introduction iv

The Writing Process 1
Prewriting
Writing
Editing (Revising)
Strengthening your style

Parts of a Professional Letter 10

Optional Parts of a Letter 16

Letter Formats 21

Creating a Professional Appearance for Your Letter 25

Preparing Professional Envelopes 27

Sample Letters

Introduction Letters 28
1. New business associate
2. New form
3. New location
4. New product/service

Thank-You Letters 32
1. Hospitality
2. Assistance
3. Customer referral
4. Gift
5. Invitation – accepting and declining

Letters of Request 37
1. Available product
2. Delivery requirement
3. "Yes" response to a request
4. "No" response to a request

Announcement Letters 41
1. New address
2. New business
3. Price increase

Sales Letters 44
1. Advertising
2. Products/programs/services
3. Follow-up

Orders 47
1. Confirming a delivery
2. Insufficient information
3. Order cancellation
4. Order change
5. Charging an order
6. Order confirmation

TABLE OF CONTENTS

Apology Letters 54
1. Delay
2. Misunderstanding
3. Accepting partial responsibility
4. Company policy doesn't allow the customer's request
5. Customer received poor service

Proposals 61
1. Contract proposal
2. Decision not yet made
3. Request for proposal
4. Proposal accepted
5. Proposal rejected

Employment Letters 66
1. Application
2. Job query
3. Recommendation
4. Follow-up letter
5. Accepting a job offer
6. Refusing a job offer
7. Resignation
8. Thank-you for interview

Adjustment Letters 76
1. Credit card billing error
2. Damage notification
3. Adjusting policy
4. Replacing merchandise

Complaint Letters 81
1. Billing error
2. Misunderstanding instructions
3. Lack of courtesy from an employee
4. Unsatisfactory performance
5. Unsatisfactory product/service

Collection Letters 86
1. Gentle reminder
2. Stronger reminder
3. Request for an explanation
4. Appeal for payment
5. Last call for payment

Sympathy Letters 91
1. Acknowledgment of sympathy letter received
2. Death
3. Terminal illness
4. Illness/injury

TABLE OF CONTENTS

Writing Effective Memos 96
    General format
    Quick tips for readable memos

Sample Memos 98
    1. Announcement of new staff member
    2. Announcement of job promotion
    3. Disappointing news for staff
    4. Notification of a team meeting
    5. Announcement of workshop
    6. Announcement of new policy
    7. Clarifying a policy change
    8. Requesting something from another department
    9. Response
    10. Reminder

Writing Effective E-mail 108
    Advantages of e-mail
    Disadvantages of e-mail

Suggestions for Using E-mail Effectively 109

E-mail Etiquette 118

Reference 119
    1. Forms of address
    2. Postal abbreviations

Recommended resources 123

INTRODUCTION

Dear Reader:

When you sit down to write, do you ever hear yourself saying, "I hate to write," "I don't know how to get started," "Why can't I just make a telephone call?" If so, you're not alone!

But there is good news — help has arrived! How? In the form of this practical manual. You will learn specific guidelines for creating business correspondence that will capture your reader's attention, encourage action, promote goodwill, and get results. You will discover ways to compose letters and memos faster by following proven techniques for planning, organizing, formatting, writing, and editing the most popular office documents. And what will be the payoff for you as a writer? You'll increase your confidence, enhance your credibility, and heighten your visibility within your organization.

In addition to writing tips and techniques, you will find sample letters, memos, and e-mail covering a variety of situations such as:

Introductions	Thank-yous	Requests	Announcements
Sales	Orders	Apologies	Proposals
Employment	Adjustments	Complaints	Collections
Sympathy			

Use these verbatim or edit them to fit your particular circumstance.

Writing clearly and concisely is a critical skill for communicating successfully in today's business environment. It's also a skill that can be enjoyable and rewarding. This manual is designed to help you achieve these results.

Here's to becoming a stronger and more effective writer. Enjoy!

Pat Cramer
Pat Cramer

Debra Smith
Debra Smith

THE WRITING PROCESS

You are about to engage in one of America's favorite organizational pastimes — writing a letter, memo, or e-mail. How do you begin? The easiest and fastest way to begin is to remember that writing is a process consisting of three stages — prewriting, writing, and editing (or revising). You can save time, reduce your stress, and make your correspondence more reader-oriented if you follow each stage.

Prewriting

A well-planned letter, memo, or e-mail depends on the clear thinking you do before you ever write your first sentence. Too often people begin to write without taking the time to consider why they are writing or who will be reading their words. Your writing will be clear only if your thinking is clear. Planning and organizing can reduce needless first, second, or third attempts at writing. These steps help clarify your thinking and improve the chance that you will get your information across to your reader. Before you put pen to paper or fingers to keyboard, consider these questions:

- Is this letter, memo, or e-mail even necessary?

- Can you make a telephone call or send a form or guide letter instead?

- What is your purpose? What do you want this document to accomplish? Is it to inform your reader? Is it to ask for information or action? Is it to persuade? Is it to propose an idea? Is it to sell a product or service? Is it to create a good impression of your organization?

- Who is your reader? Consider such factors as age, gender, position, education, knowledge of subject, personality style, interest level, biases, and reaction to your subject. For example, have you corresponded on this subject before? What does your reader want or need? When? Why? How much does your reader already know? How can you help your reader? Do you expect your reader to reply? How? When?

- What are the key points to cover? Once you know your purpose and have visualized your reader, take time to think through your ideas. Just jot down a word or two on each key point that needs to be covered. You can go back later and put them in the best order.

- What do you want your reader to do? What response or action do you expect from your reader? For example, do you want your reader to read your letter and file it? Read it and toss it? Read it and take action? Read it and pass it on to another reader? If you want your reader to call you, do you say, "Please call me by 3:00 on Friday" or do you say, "Please contact me this week"?

Whatever response or action you want from your reader, be sure to state it at the end of your letter or memo and be specific. Don't assume your reader can read your mind. Only you can do that!

But what if you suffer from a common disease known as "writer's block"? It's the moment when you are sitting in front of your computer screen or notepad, and nothing comes to mind. The blank screen or paper stares back at you, and you feel yourself becoming desperate! You can use any of these techniques to reduce your panic and engage your brain:

- Talking it out — Imagine what you would say if you were talking to your reader over the telephone or face to face. Write what you would say in your conversation. You can always go back and polish your language later.

- Listing — List the ideas you think you should include in your document.

> Words are the best medium of exchange of thoughts and ideas between people.
>
> — William Ross

Sequence them in the order you will cover them. Then turn the ideas into complete thoughts.

- Outlining — Remember your high-school days when you were composing those book reports and term papers? If outlining worked then, it will work now.

  I. _____
    A. _____
      1. _____
        a. _____
        b. _____
      2. _____
        a. _____
        b. _____
    B. _____
    C. _____
  II. _____

- 5 W's and 1 H — To get started, answer each of these questions: who, what, where, when, why, and how. If you give your reader no other information except the answers to these questions, you will have conveyed the most important ideas.

- Clustering or Mind Mapping — Consider using this "right brain" approach. Start by drawing a circle in the center of your page. Write the purpose of your letter or memo in the circle. Then generate your main ideas and place them in smaller circles connected by straight lines to your main circle. As you create sub-ideas to the main ideas, you can show those in an even smaller set of circles that are connected by straight lines to the second tier of circles. Once you finish creating your ideas, then put them in a logical order.

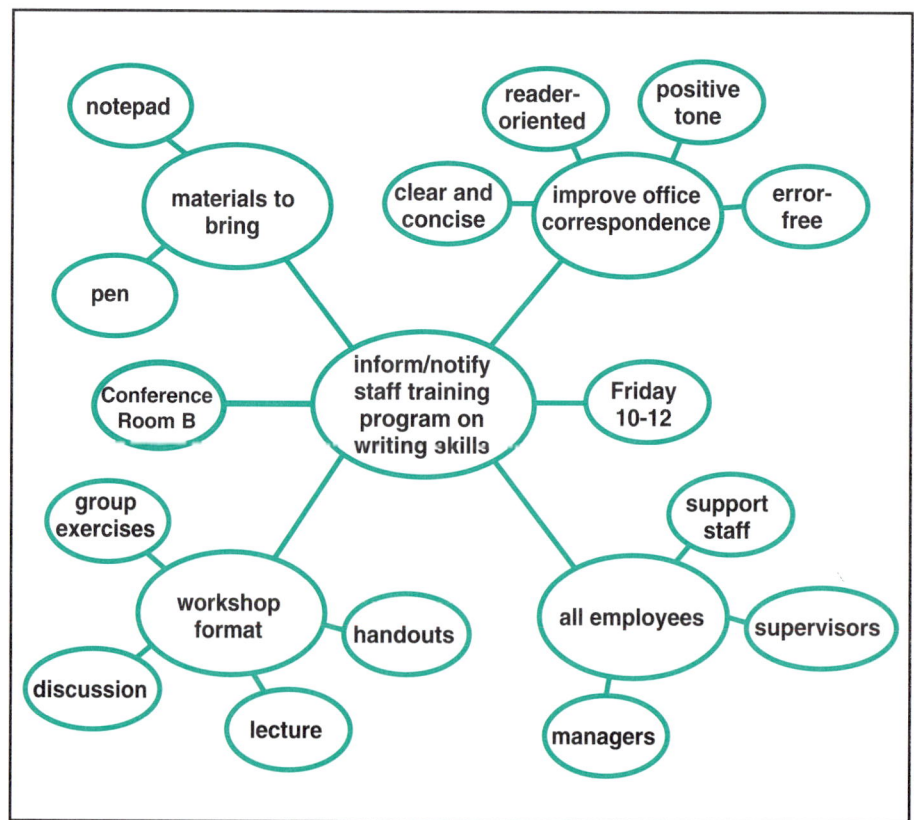

Clustering or Mind Mapping approach

Writing

Once you plan and organize your ideas, then it's time to turn them into sentences and paragraphs. In this stage, your purpose is to write a rough draft — not a perfect piece. Don't worry about grammar, punctuation, spelling, usage, capitalization, or word choice. You can always go back and correct any errors you've made. At this point, composing is more important than cleaning up.

Editing (Revising)

Now is the time to review your rough draft and polish it. How do you do this? Read it and check for organization, sentence structure, spelling, usage, grammar, punctuation, and capitalization.

- Have unnecessary words and phrases been eliminated?
- Are dates, numbers, names, and facts accurate?
- Are sentences complete?
- Do subjects and verbs agree?
- Have archaic words, jargon, and redundancies been removed?
- Is the purpose stated at the beginning?
- Is your document reader-oriented?
- Is the desired action stated clearly?
- Do the sentences flow logically and smoothly?
- Do the paragraphs flow logically and smoothly?
- Have all the reader's questions been answered?
- Is active voice used more than passive voice?
- Is the writing conversational?
- Is the tone appropriate?

You can minimize errors and costly mistakes if you spend less time writing and more time revising. Rather than strive for perfection, just get your ideas on paper. Then go back and polish them. Here are some suggestions:

- Take a recess, then go back to your writing and read it aloud. You will be more aware if your sentences are too long, if subjects and verbs agree, if your choice of tense is appropriate, etc.
- Schedule critical input from others. Have another person review your letter, memo, or e-mail.
- Pretend you are the reader and critique your own writing.
- Check your content — facts, statistics, dates, and amounts.
- Check the basics — smooth transitions, verbs, jargon, wordiness, and visual layout.
- Edit ruthlessly — sound advice from Malcolm Forbes!

> There are only two tests for telling whether a letter is too long. One is whether it says more than need be said. The other is whether it takes too many words to say it.
>
> — Mona Sheppard

Strengthening Your Style
Following the three stages of writing—prewriting, writing, and editing—certainly will assist you in creating high-impact letters, memos, and e-mail. In addition, these style suggestions will help you achieve clarity and conciseness and convey the right tone.

1. Use short, simple words
   (or, deflate inflated language).

One of the major causes of wordy, unclear writing is the use of inflated words instead of simple ones. For instance, some writers take a simple word like "end" and dress it up so it becomes "terminate." Inflated words may have the same meaning, but they clutter your writing, confuse your reader, and make your writing sound phony and stilted. No one appreciates having to read a business letter with a dictionary in one hand.

Inflated	Simple and natural
procure	get
endeavor	try
utilization	use
metropolis	city
disseminate	spread
substantiate	support

Does this mean you should never use big words? Certainly not! The key is to use them at the appropriate time and direct them to the appropriate reader. If your reader uses long, multisyllable words, you can also use them. When in doubt, use a short, simple word, rather than a long, complex one.

2. Eliminate wordy expressions.

Wordy expressions are needless phrases often introduced by prepositions like *at, on, for, in, to,* and *by*. They don't give your sentences impressive bulk; they weaken them by cluttering the words that do carry the meaning. So cut the deadwood! The longer you take to say something, the weaker you come across. Getting rid of these stuffy habit phrases makes your writing more natural and friendly.

Wordy	Simple and clear
due to the fact that	because
in order to	to
in the amount of $50	for $50
in the city of Austin	in Austin
during periods when	when
by means of	by
at the present time	now
prior to the start of	before

3. Remove redundancies.

Redundancies are words that say the same thing twice. They are a sign of careless thinking. Redundancies are hard to spot because you often hear them in everyday conversation.

Redundant	Better
refer back	refer
fill out and complete	complete
definite decision	decision
plan ahead	plan
very unique	unique
advance warning	warning
qualified expert	expert
still remains	remains
totally destroyed	destroyed
postpone until later	postpone
merge together	merge
personal opinion	opinion

4. Avoid clichés.

Learn to recognize and remove trite expressions and clichés from your writing. Beware: They often lurk in beginnings and endings. Replace them with crisp and original language.

Outdated and overused	Updated
enclosed please find	enclosed is
please be advised that	(omit)
this office is in receipt of your letter	thank you for your letter
as per your request	regarding your request
please do not hesitate to contact	please call
please feel free to call	please call
thanking you in advance for your cooperation	thank you for your
hoping to hear from you soon	I would appreciate hearing from you by (date)

Knowing you want to use simple words, eliminate wordy expressions, remove redundancies, and avoid clichés, which letter would you prefer to receive?

Dear Mr. Weitzel:

Per your letter, enclosed please find the information regarding the materials you conveyed interest in procuring. Due to the fact that few supplies still remain at the present time in our warehouse department, it is of the utmost importance and significance that you fill out and complete the attached order form as soon as possible.

We appreciate your patronage, and thank you in advance for your support.

Dear Mr. Weitzel:

Here's the information you requested about our product. Since quantities are limited, please complete and return the attached order form by June 10. You can expect delivery by June 24.

Thank you for your order.

Writing clearly and concisely

Notice how the second letter sounds more conversational, clear, and concise — characteristics of good writing.

5. Avoid archaic, technical, and legalistic jargon.

One of the greatest enemies of natural, sincere writing is the use of archaic, technical, or legalistic jargon. Archaic words and phrases may have been acceptable 50 years ago, but they are not appreciated today. They only serve to make your letters cold, impersonal, pompous, and unnatural.

Old-fashioned	Modern
this writer	I
duly noted	received, seen
find herewith	enclosed
kindly	please
pursuant to our agreement	as we agreed

Technical jargon is the language of a particular profession or group. Before using it, know who your reader will be. Be careful that it doesn't slip in unnoticed because it comes so naturally to you. Also, don't use acronyms in your writing without explaining them first.

Equally confusing are overuse and inappropriate use of legal terms. Some writers use legalisms in the hope of adding importance to their message. But be careful — they can make your writing stuffy and cold. For example, what's your reaction to this letter?

> Dear Mr. Wang:
>
> Hereinbelow set forth are two copies of the report attendant to your purchase of the duplex. Although said report has been revised pursuant to your request, we nonetheless deem it advisable for you to re-examine paragraph 4 as per our agreement.

Eliminating archaic jargon

6. Use gender-neutral language.

To avoid ignoring one of the sexes, use gender-neutral terms.

Instead of	Use
mankind	people
to man	to staff, operate
salesman	sales representative
fireman	firefighter

Consider these other suggestions for staying clear of sexist language:

- Rewrite your sentences in the plural.

From: Each manager must submit his status report.

To: Managers must submit their status reports.

- Address your reader in the second person.

From: The candidate must complete his application by Tuesday.

To: Complete your application by Tuesday.

- Avoid using pronouns whenever possible.

From: Each pharmacist must pass a board examination before he becomes licensed.

To: Each pharmacist must pass a board examination before being licensed.

7. Keep your verbs active.

Verbs are the heart of your sentences. They can be active or passive. When you write in the active voice, the subject of your sentence performs the action. When you write in the passive voice, the subject of your sentence is acted upon or receives the action.

Active: We studied the report.

Passive: A study of the report was made by us.

Active: The manufacturers confirmed that they inspect the merchandise before shipping.

Passive: It was confirmed by the manufacturers that inspection of the merchandise prior to shipping is made by them.

As a general rule, active verbs have more life, acknowledge responsibility, and are more personal. Passive verbs make your sentences wordy and roundabout, muddle your meaning, and sound unnatural and dull.

8. Unsmother your verbs.

Strong working verbs are the backbone of English sentences. They are what make your sentences move. They put action into writing, so why take a useful, hardworking verb, make it into a noun, and add a lifeless substitute verb? For example, "choose" becomes "make a choice." Avoid smothering verbs by watching for words that end in:

-ive	indicative	indicate
-sion	decision	decide
-ment	development	develop
-tion	consideration	consider

Another tip-off that you are smothering verbs is overuse of the words *make, give, take,* and *come.*

take under consideration	consider
make a quotation	quote
come to the realization	realize
make a presentation	present

Caution: Smothered verbs and passive construction often go together. When they do, you are out to punish your reader.

9. Strive for short sentences.

Short sentences add strength, vitality, and clarity to your writing. Just how long should a sentence be? It should be long enough to get your message across, yet short enough to be vigorous. Most people can comfortably read sentences of 15 to 20 words or fewer. As the number of words grows, reading becomes more difficult. If you are averaging sentences of 35 to 40 words, your reader will probably have to read your letter two or three times to understand your message. So follow these tips for keeping your sentences short and manageable.

- Keep the average sentence length to 15 to 20 words or fewer.

- Limit each sentence to one main idea.

- Break a long sentence (25 words or more) into two sentences. Often a period can replace *ands*, *buts*, and other conjunctions that run two sentences together. A simple, readable sentence avoids rambling ideas and multiple clauses.

- Vary the length of your sentences, occasionally using a sentence of five or six words or fewer.

- Use a connective (*and*, *but*, etc.) to start a new sentence.

- Occasional long sentences are fine, provided they flow smoothly and are well-punctuated.

10. Keep related words together.

One especially good tip for writing clearly is to keep related sentence elements together and unrelated sentence elements apart. Watch for misplaced modifiers — words, phrases, or clauses that are placed next to the wrong word in a sentence. You generally can correct this confusion by placing the modifier next to the word it is meant to describe.

Misplaced: No reference manuals will be given to administrative assistants that are *out of date*.

Better: No *out-of-date* reference manuals will be given to administrative assistants.

Misplaced: Please report to Security that the delivery truck parked behind the main building *is out of gas*.

Better: Please report to Security that the delivery truck, which *is out of gas*, is parked behind the main building.

11. Avoid unclear references.

You may know what you are saying and meaning in your sentences, but that doesn't mean your reader will. Make sure pronouns refer clearly to their subjects. If they don't, invest the time to rewrite the sentence.

Unclear: Dale explained to Fred that he would be conducting the meeting on Friday.

Clear: Dale asked Fred to conduct the meeting on Friday.

Unclear: The sales manager could not answer any questions, and the sales rep was uncooperative. This can hurt your business.

Clear: The sales manager could not answer any questions, and the sales rep was uncooperative. This poor service can result in lost customers and profit.

12. Keep your tone positive.

Courtesy in a business letter or memo is vital even when you are saying no to your reader. Words are like people. They have personalities too. Some are dry and dull; some confusing and vague; some positive or negative. Be aware of the emotional tones of the words you use.

Negative	Positive
it is obvious	we have noticed
you must	please
you have to	we ask that
it is our policy to	our practice is
you can't	you can
you claim that	you mentioned, stated

Whenever possible, emphasize the good news, not the bad. Tell your readers what they can do, not what they cannot do. When you soften unpleasant ideas with positive wording, you'll receive a more positive response from your reader. Notice the difference in the tone of these next two letters.

HOW TO CREATE HIGH-IMPACT LETTERS, MEMOS, AND E-MAIL

Dear Ms. Bell:

It has come to my attention that you are delinquent in your payment of $165.83. Your lack of financial responsibility cannot and will not be tolerated by our company. If you do not remit your check by October 29, we will be forced to pursue legal action against you. It is our policy that customers meet their obligations to us or suffer the consequences.

Dear Ms. Bell:

So that you can maintain your credit with us, please send your payment of $165.83 by October 29. We want to continue working with you and providing you with the service you have come to expect from us.

Thank you for making the payment.

Remember, it's not just what you say but how you say it.

Using a positive tone

We have examined the writing process and looked at ways to strengthen style. In the next section, we'll explore the essential parts of a letter.

PARTS OF A PROFESSIONAL LETTER

Letterhead
(first page only) ....

> **INNOVATIVE TRAINING CORPORATION**
> 329 Garcon Lane • Los Angeles, CA 91420

1. Date .... October 14, 199x

Ms. Sherilyn Watt
Department of Economic Affairs
2. Inside address .... 1709 37th Avenue
Paso Robles, CA 93446

3. Salutation .... Dear Ms. Watt:

Thank you for your request for information about working with your team to develop a positive office environment. After reviewing your needs assessment results and conducting several focus groups, I agree that we have an opportunity for change.

The staff members seem willing to explore more effective ways of creating collaborative outcomes, and your departmental goals and objectives certainly support team-building training.

4. Body .... Let's agree on a short-term plan. I suggest that we conduct two additional focus group meetings and approximately 12 individual interviews. At that point, you and I can review the data gathered, and I will design a six-hour training program, as you requested. You will have input into both the outline and the finished workshop material, with appropriate changes made at each review.

The design and training fees will remain as we have already agreed, and the follow-up report will be included at no additional charge. If you have further questions, please call me at xxx-xxxx. I am looking forward to working with you to create a highly productive team.

5. Complimentary close .... Sincerely,

6. Signature line .... Caroline Alexander
Senior consultant

The various parts of the letter detailed below will help set a standard of uniformity within an office. When everyone follows the same format, you will create a very professional image.

1. Date

- The usual method is MONTH, DAY, YEAR. Use: March 21, 1998

- Formal business letters do not abbreviate the month. Not: Mar. 21, 1998

- Informal internal documents (such as team reports and informal memos) sometimes use abbreviations or shortened forms.

Use: Mar. 21, 1998 or 3-21-98 or 3/21/98

- Military offices or governmental agencies often reverse the order. Many countries other than the United States prefer this format, and it simplifies the work for two reasons: the punctuation is eliminated, which saves keystrokes, and it is easier to use with a numerical filing system. Use: 21 March 1998

- Dates are typed approximately two inches from the top of the page (usually line 13), or three lines below the letterhead.

> Don't write merely to be understood. Write so that you cannot possibly be misunderstood.
>
> — Robert Louis Stevenson

2. Inside address

Use: Addressee name
 Addressee title and
  department (if applicable)
 Organization name
 Street address
  (number and name)
 City, State, ZIP Code

Note: The U.S. Postal Service prefers the title of the recipient above the organization's name.

- Normally, the inside address starts on the sixth line below the date. However, this may be adjusted for proper alignment in window envelopes, or increased or decreased for very long or very short letters.

- Do not use an inside address in a personal letter.

- Single-space the inside address, aligned at the left margin.

- If you are sending the same letter to two or more people at different addresses, type them one under the other (with one space between) or position them professionally side by side. On the envelope for each recipient, type the individual name only, omitting reference to the other recipients.

- **Be careful!** Misspellings are a disaster! Always spell the name of the addressee correctly; call for the correct spelling if you are unsure.

- If the addressee's name, title, or company name is quite long, place each of them on a separate line.
 Use: Ms. Suzanne VanHartsinger
  Northeastern Sales Manager
  Blessing Co. Inc.

- Ordinarily, do not use an academic degree with an inside address.

Numbers used in street addresses have some variation:
- Spell out numbers one through ten.
 Use: 2135 Third Avenue

- Type figures/numerals for street numbers higher than ten.
 Use: 4791 East 77th Street

- When a compass direction appears *before* a street name, do not abbreviate it (unless space is limited).
 Use: 345 West Ninth Street

If the compass direction appears *after* the street name, follow the locally preferred style. If there aren't any special preferences, do the following:

INNOVATIVE TRAINING CORPORATION
329 Garcon Lane • Los Angeles, CA 91420

October 14, 199x

Ms. Sherilyn Watt
Department of Economic Affairs
1709 37th Avenue
Paso Robles, CA 93446

Dear Ms. Watt:

Thank you for your request for information about working with your team to develop a positive office environment. After reviewing your needs assessment results and conducting several focus groups, I agree that we have an opportunity for change.

The staff members seem willing to explore more effective ways of creating collaborative outcomes, and your departmental goals and objectives certainly support team-building training.

Let's agree on a short-term plan. I suggest that we conduct two additional focus group meetings and approximately 12 individual interviews. At that point, you and I can review the data gathered, and I will design a six-hour training program, as you requested. You will have input into both the outline and the finished workshop material, with appropriate changes made at each review.

The design and training fees will remain as we have already agreed, and the follow-up report will be included at no additional charge. If you have further questions, please call me at xxx-xxxx. I am looking forward to working with you to create a highly productive team.

Sincerely,

Caroline Alexander
Senior consultant

- Abbreviate a compound direction that is a section of a city. Do not use a period after, but do use a comma before.
 Use: 1414 Grant Street, SW

- Spell out *North*, *South*, *East*, and *West* following a street name, and don't use a comma.
 Use: 131 Central Park West

- A post office box number is frequently used instead of an address.
 Use: P.O. Box 1127
  Post Office Box 1127
  Box 1127

3. Salutation

- Align the salutation at the left margin, on the second line below the inside address. Follow it with a colon.

- While formal business style uses the colon with a reader's last name, you may use a comma if you have typed the reader's first name.
  Use: Dear Ms. Swanson:
  Or: Dear Elizabeth,

- You may abbreviate the titles Mr., Mrs., Ms., and Dr. Spell out other titles, such as "Professor," "Bishop," "Judge," "Father," or "Sister."

- "Dear Sir" or "Gentlemen" as a salutation is not acceptable in today's business letters. In an extremely formal situation, you may use "Dear Sir or Madam," or "Ladies and Gentlemen," although it is not generally preferred. Referring to the reader by title (e.g., Dear Customer Service Representative) is much more professional, or using a simplified style that offers a subject line rather than a salutation may be a better choice.

- "To Whom It May Concern" is a poor choice for a salutation, since it appears rather outdated. Instead, use a title or a subject/attention line. But keep in mind your letter has the best shot at getting personal attention if you research the name of the person who should receive your letter.

- Use a reader's name wherever possible, although a title is a second-best option where the name is unknown.

- If a reader's name is gender-neutral (such as Dana, Chris, Pat, Terry, Robin, etc.) or initials have been given (e.g., J.L. Parker), simply use the name or initials offered.
  Use: Dear J.L. Parker:
  Or: Dear Chris Patterson:

- Where two people are being addressed, always use the word "and" instead of an ampersand (&).
  Use: Dear Mr. Ellison and
         Ms. Griffith:
  Not: Dear Mr. Ellison &
         Ms. Griffith:

4. Body of the letter

This part of the letter contains your message. You have several options about the layout of this main part of the document. These will be detailed in the section of this manual on letter styles.

The text begins on the second line below the salutation (or the second line below the subject line, if used).

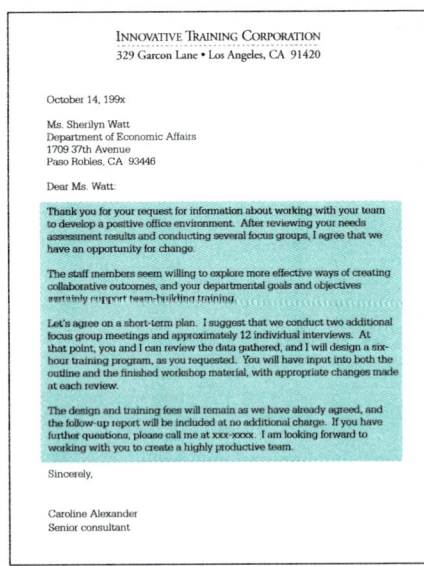

5. Complimentary closing

The complimentary closing is a polite way of ending your letter using a standard formula.

- Place your complimentary closing on the second line below the last line in the body of the letter. Follow it with a comma.

- The most common complimentary closings used today are:
  Sincerely,
  Cordially,

- Avoid these outdated closings:
  Very truly yours,
  Sincerely yours,
  Yours very truly,
  Kindest personal regards,
  Respectfully yours,
  Cordially yours,
  Your humble and obedient servant,

Informal closings are acceptable if you have an established relationship with the reader. In these situations, *Warm regards* or *Best regards* is acceptable and is followed by a comma.

6. Signature line
   (writer's name and title)

- Type the writer's name four lines below the complimentary closing. (On very short letters you may expand this space to six blank lines, while very long letters may use just two lines.)

- Include any relevant title, as well as the department where the writer works, and arrange these on two or three lines in a way that is visually pleasing.

- Special titles (such as academic degree or military rank) should appear after the name, not in front of it.
  Marjorie O'Brien, M.D.
  Peter D'Onofrio, D.O.
  Bennett L. Stevens, Colonel, USAF

- People typically do not use courtesy titles unless the name is gender neutral or initials are used:
  Sincerely,
  Mr. Kelly Cummings
  Kelly Cummings

  Cordially,
  Ms. S. Taylor
  S. Taylor

- Women will be given the courtesy title of Ms. unless they specify in either a typed or handwritten signature that they wish to be addressed differently:
  Sincerely,
  Ms. Allison Petrie
  Allison Petrie

- If two people are signing a letter, signature blocks may be typed either side by side or one below the other.

- If the side-by-side method is used, place the complimentary closing aligned with the left margin (for all letter styles), and place one signature block at the left margin, the other at the center.

- If the one above/one below method is used, type the second block four lines below the end of the first block, at either the left margin or the center, depending on the letter style.

INNOVATIVE TRAINING CORPORATION
329 Garcon Lane • Los Angeles, CA 91420

October 14, 199x

Ms. Sherilyn Watt
Department of Economic Affairs
1709 37th Avenue
Paso Robles, CA 93446

Dear Ms. Watt:

Thank you for your request for information about working with your team to develop a positive office environment. After reviewing your needs assessment results and conducting several focus groups, I agree that we have an opportunity for change.

The staff members seem willing to explore more effective ways of creating collaborative outcomes, and your departmental goals and objectives certainly support team-building training.

Let's agree on a short-term plan. I suggest that we conduct two additional focus group meetings and approximately 12 individual interviews. At that point, you and I can review the data gathered, and I will design a six-hour training program, as you requested. You will have input into both the outline and the finished workshop material, with appropriate changes made at each review.

The design and training fees will remain as we have already agreed, and the follow-up report will be included at no additional charge. If you have further questions, please call me at xxx-xxxx. I am looking forward to working with you to create a highly productive team.

Sincerely,

Caroline Alexander
Senior consultant

OPTIONAL PARTS OF A LETTER

1. Special notations
2. Subject line
3. Reference initials
4. Enclosure notation
5. Delivery identification
6. Copy notation
7. Postscript

INNOVATIVE TRAINING CORPORATION

329 Garcon Lane • Los Angeles, CA 91420

October 14, 199x

REFERENCE: Project TMX-312

Ms. Sherilyn Watt
Department of Economic Affairs
1709 37th Avenue
Paso Robles, CA 93446

Dear Ms. Watt:

SUBJECT: Request for Team-Building Training

Thank you for your request for information about working with your team to develop a positive office environment. I suggest that we conduct a six-hour training program, as you requested. You will have input into both the outline and the finished workshop material, with appropriate changes made at each review.

I am looking forward to working with you to create a highly productive team.

Sincerely,

Caroline Alexander
Senior consultant

CRA/jln

Enclosure

By FedEx

cc: Barbara Brinkley

PS: I'll see you at lunch on Friday.

1. Special notations

When letters are personal or confidential, that fact can be noted directly under the date, at the left margin. The most common way is to type the notation in capital letters or in upper/lower case, underscored.

Use: PERSONAL or
CONFIDENTIAL

Or: Personal or Confidential

Another option, for those who use enhanced text functions, is to type in boldface print without underscoring.

Use: **PERSONAL** or
CONFIDENTIAL

Or: **Personal** or
Confidential

When you need to provide a reference number, type a reference notation two lines below the date or two lines below any other notation that follows a date.

Use: Refer to: Policy #4412309
Reference: Patient #257-0812
Refer to: Order #10078

These reference numbers are often used with insurance policies, bank or credit card accounts, orders, medical or hospital records, student identifications, etc.

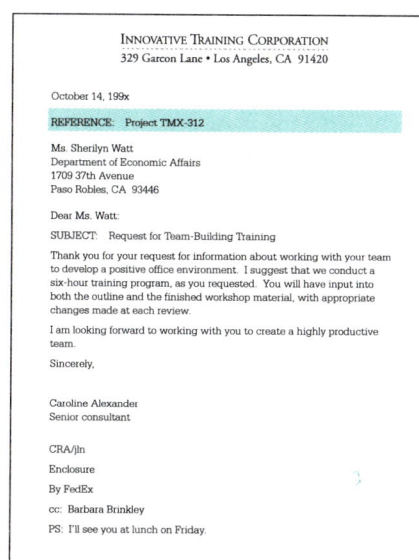

2. Subject line

The subject line is often omitted, except in the simplified style, where it replaces the salutation of the letter. Many experts think that it is a courtesy to the reader to indicate the contents and assist in creating a frame of reference. This is a logical consideration, since many poorly written letters don't clearly state a purpose up front, and confused readers are left wondering, "Why am I reading this?" A subject line eliminates any confusion and signals to a reader whether this letter is of interest.

- A subject line aligns with the left margin, unless indented paragraphs are used, in which case the subject line is indented the same number of spaces.

- With simplified style, where no salutation is used, a subject line is typed on the second line below the inside address.

- With all other types of letters, the optional subject line appears between the salutation and the body of the letter with one blank line above it and one below.

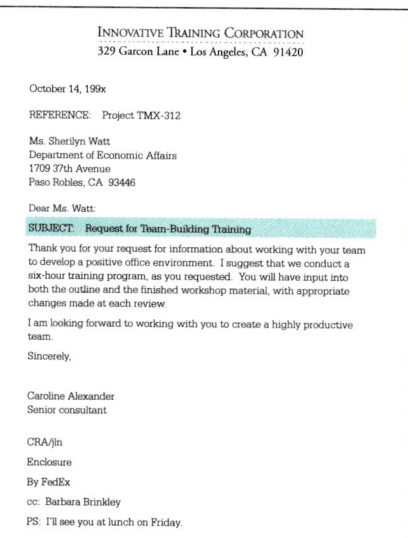

3. Reference initials

- The easiest reference identifier when the writer's name is placed in the signature block is to provide the typist's initials alone in small letters.

- Place these initials two lines below the writer's name and title. If the writer's initials are used as well, they are always given first.

- You may type both sets of initials the same way if you wish, either all capital letters or all small letters. You may use either a diagonal slash or a colon.

  ERD/JNL   erd/jnl
  ERD:JNL   erd:jnl

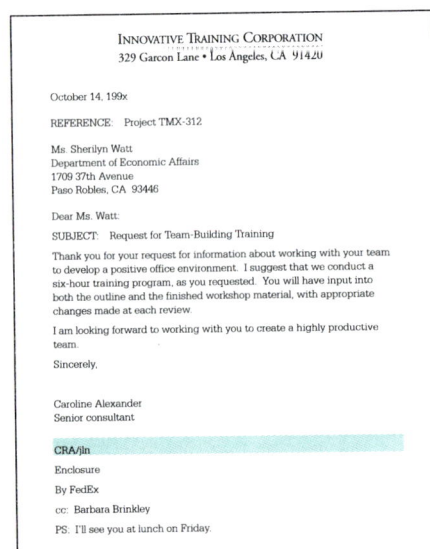

4. Enclosure notation

Sometimes writers wish to highlight for a reader that specific information has been included with the letter. This courtesy alerts the reader to not discard other loose pieces with the packaging or envelope. Simply type the word "Enclosure" or another abbreviation at the left margin, two lines below the reference initials.

Use: Enclosure: (describe)
         Encl: (describe)
         Enc: (describe)

- The description is optional and can consist of a number indicating the quantity of enclosures or a more detailed description. Use a colon between the word enclosure and any detail.

- Be sure that the number of enclosures named in the letter matches what has been included. Readers are frustrated if they think they did not receive something that should have been enclosed.

- The word "Attachment" can be used as an alternative to "Enclosure."

- If additional material is being sent separately, use the term "Separate cover" or "Under separate cover" and identify the item being sent.

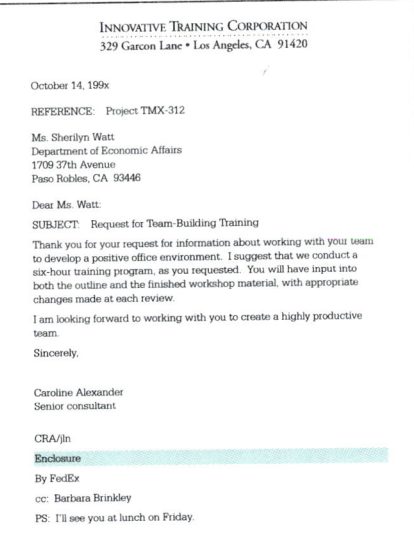

5. Delivery identification

When a business letter will be sent by means other than first-class U.S. mail, an identification is often placed two lines below the Enclosure reference or the reference initials, whichever appears last. State specifically the method of delivery:

By fax
By Priority Mail
By Federal Express or By FedEx
By messenger
By certified mail
By Special Delivery
By Express Mail

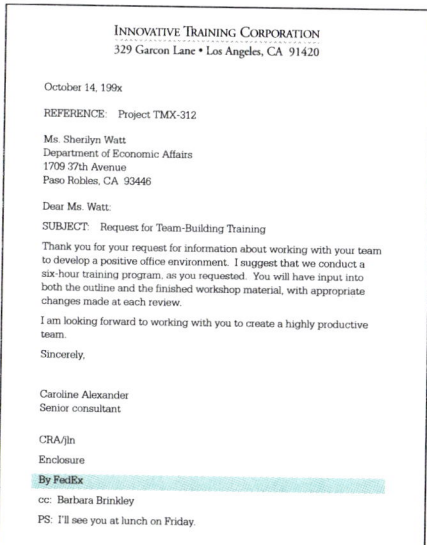

6. Copy notation

Copy notations are important to let readers know who else will receive the material. Meant as a courtesy, they can also create an historical record identifying who has been part of a communication chain and is therefore aware of previous issues, requests, or problems. Sometimes the "cc" notation is used for political purposes, such as documentation. The traditional term "cc" (which used to indicate "carbon copy") is still used to mean "courtesy copy," or simply "copies" in the plural. Some writers don't like to use the term "cc"; others have no problem with it. Alternatives exist for those who object to "cc":

Use: c:
       Copy to: (or Copies to:)
       Distribution:

Avoid: pc: (used to mean photocopy)

- Type the copy identification on the second line below the reference initials, enclosure notation, or delivery identification, whichever comes last.

- List the recipients in ranked order (if this is important in the organization being addressed) or simply in alphabetical order.

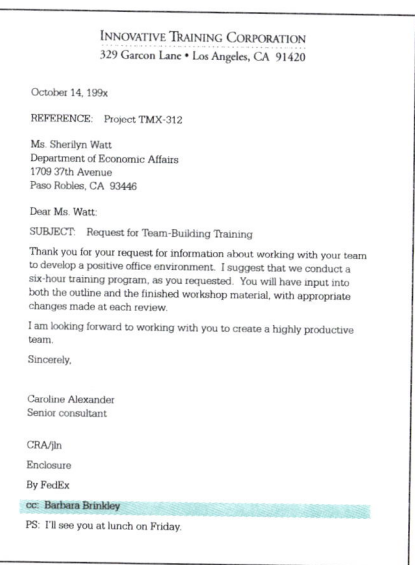

- You may type the copy notation with or without a colon.

- Omit courtesy titles (Ms./Mr.) in a copy reference if first names or initials are used with the last names.

- A "blind copy" notation (bc) is used for copies that are being sent to additional recipients without the addressee's knowledge. Place the "bc" reference on the "blind" copies, but *not* on the original or the cc's.

The file copy of the letter should list *all* blind copy notations (which are usually removed on any other copies made in the future).

- The writer does not have to personally sign additional copies of the letter (unless it would appear cold and distant to the specific reader, in which case a brief handwritten note is appropriate).

- Normally, when a letter has both a copy notation and an enclosure notation, everyone assumes that enclosures were sent with the *original* letter only. If, in fact, enclosures were sent with copies, simply type next to the name what that reader received.

7. Postscript

A postscript (PS) is used for an afterthought or a personal comment, or to provide emphasis for an idea that does not have to be included in the body of the letter. Don't put any critical information or anything that the reader would have wanted to know earlier in a postscript, or the letter will seem very disorganized. A PS can be an effective tool to highlight a particular idea or to leave a powerful final impression or an intriguing thought. It is not frequently used in formal letters, but is quite popular with marketing and advertising pieces. It is also used in chatty, informal letters because of its casual tone.

- Traditionally, the abbreviation for postscript was P.S. The more common way to type it today is PS.

- Begin a PS on the second line below the last typed reference or notation.

- Use the notation "PS:" or "PS." followed by two spaces.

- Use this letter feature sparingly. It loses its power when written inappropriately.

LETTER FORMATS

"Full block" format
- All lines begin at the left margin.
- Nothing is indented, unless it is a quotation, graph, table etc.
- This is the style most commonly used in word processing.

———— Letterhead ————

Date

Inside address
jdakjiejal a iejal djkdji
euivnei ieowjwjl
wojvle aijewilsjfml

Salutation:

jdakjiejal a iejal djkdji euivnei ieowjwjl wojvle aijewi lsjfml woj eui djkdji euivne kjiejal a ie ojvle aije kjiejal a ieja kdji eudji euivnvle aijewi lsjfm. jdakjiejal a iejal djkdji euivnei ieowjwjl wojvle aijewi lsjfml woj eui djkdji euivne kjiejal a ie ojvle aije kjiejal a ieja kdji eudji euivnvle aijewi lsjfm.

jdakjiejal a iejal djkdji euivnei ieowjwjl wojvle aijewi lsjfml woj eui djkdji euivne kjiejal a ie ojvle aije kjiejal a ieja kdji eudji euivnvle aijewi lsjfm a iejal djkdji e jwjl wojvle aijewi lsjfml woj eui owjwjl wojvle ivnei ieow.

Complimentary closing,

Signature and title

Reference initials

"Modified block"
— standard style format

- This is still one of the most popular letter formats.

- All of the lines begin at the left margin, except the date, complimentary closing, and writer's signature and title, which begin at the center.

———————— Letterhead ————————

Date

Inside address
jdakjiejal a iejal djkdji
euivnei ieowjwjl
wojvle aijewilsjfml

Salutation:

jdakjiejal a iejal djkdji euivnei ieowjwjl wojvle aijewi lsjfml woj eui djkdji euivne kjiejal a ie ojvle aije kjiejal a ieja kdji eudji euivnvle aijewi lsjfm uivn djkdj.

jdakjiejal a iejal djkdji euivnei ieowjwjl wojvle aijewi lsjfml woj eui djkdji euivne kjiejal a ie ojvle aije kjiejal a ieja kdji eudji euivnvle aijewi lsjfm.

jdakjiejal a iejal djkdji euivnei ieowjwjl wojvle aijewi lsjfml woj eui wojvle ivnei ieow.

                                            Complimentary closing,

                                            Signature and title

Reference initials

Enclosure

Copy notation

"Modified block"
— indented style format
This letter style is identical to the standard style described at left except that the first line of every paragraph is indented one-half inch, or approximately five spaces. Sometimes this is called semi-block style.

———— Letterhead ————

Date

Inside address
jdakjiejal a iejal djkdji
euivnei ieowjwjl
wojvle aijewilsjfml

Salutation:

    jdakjiejal a iejal djkdji euivnei ieowjwjl wojvle aijewi lsjfml woj eui djkdji euivne kjiejal a ie ojvle aije kjiejal a ieja kdji eudji euivnvle aijewi lsjfm uivn djkdj.

    jdakjiejal a iejal djkdji euivnei ieowjwjl wojvle aijewi lsjfml woj euidj kdji euivne kjiejal a ie ojvle aije kjiejal a ieja kdji eudji euivnvle aijewi lsjfm.

    jdakjiejal a iejal djkdji euivnei ieowjwjl wojvle aijewi lsjfml woj eui wojvle ivnei ieow.

    Complimentary closing,

    Signature and title

Enclosure

    PS: ivne kjiejal a ie ojvle aije kjiejal a ieja kdji.

Simplified format

This format is sometimes referred to as the AMS format because it has been recommended by the Administrative Management Society.

- All lines begin at the left margin.
- The salutation is replaced by a subject line typed in capital letters.
- The complimentary closing is omitted.
- The writer's identification is typed in capital letters on one line, following the signature.

Letterhead

Date

Inside address
jdakjiejal a iejal djkdji
euivnei ieowjwjl
wojvle aijewilsjfml

SUBJECT LINE

jdakjiejal a iejal djkdji euivnei ieowjwjl wojvle aijewi lsjfml woj eui djkdji euivne kjiejal a ie ojvle aije kjiejal a ieja kdji eudji euivnvle aijewi lsjfm uivn djkdjal a iejal djkdji euivnei ieowjwjl wojvle aijewi lsjf laie ojvle ai.

jdakjiejal a iejal djkdji euivnei ieowjwjl wojvle aijewi lsjfml woj euidj kdji euivne kjiejal a ie ojvle aije kjiejal a ieja kdji eudji euivnvle aijewi lsjtm djkdj1 euivne kjiejal a ie ojvlo aije kjiejal a ieja kdji eudji euivnvle jvle aije kjiejal.

jdakjiejal a iejal djkdji euivnei ieowjwjl wojvle aijewi lsjfml woj eui wojvle ivnei ieow jal a iejal djkdji euivnei ieowjwjl wojvle aijewi lsjfml woj euidj kdji euivne kjiejal a ie ojvle aije kjiejal a ieja kdji eudji euivnv vle ivnei ieow jal a ie i lsjfml.

WRITER'S NAME, TITLE

Reference initials

CREATING A PROFESSIONAL APPEARANCE FOR YOUR LETTER

The way a letter looks initially and the "first impression" it creates are critical to positive acceptance from the reader. A business writer must consider the margins, spacing, print font, paragraph length, individual sentence length, and "white space." Balance is important! A shorter letter may need to be "stretched" with a larger font and slightly wider margins rather than leaving a huge block of empty space at the bottom. A longer letter could extend to additional pages rather than being crammed into a tight place with narrow margins and no white space to relax the eye.

Typical letter positioning
- Center the letter horizontally on the page with uniform margins.
- Shorter paragraphs are easier for the reader to understand and absorb.
- In more formal letters, section headings or titles may be used to identify the content of individual paragraphs.
- When indenting your paragraphs, set your tab for five to seven spaces (about a half inch).
- Always double-space between paragraphs, regardless of the format being used.

Top margins
- With letterhead stationery, type the date (always the first letter feature to be used) three lines below the letterhead.
- With plain stationery, type the date on the first line below the two-inch top margin.
- Use a one-inch top margin on every continuation (following) page of a letter. Remember, these pages are always plain stationery, regardless of what is used on the first page.

Bottom margins
- Always use a bottom margin of at least one inch. If the letter will run two pages or more, increase the bottom margin on the first page to two inches.
- If your letterhead has printed copy across the bottom (a "band"), always leave at least a half-inch margin between that and the bottom line of typed copy.

Left and right margins
- Check your computer software first to see what preset (default) margin has been created. Some software programs use 1.25 inches, but most use one inch. This gives you a 6.5-inch text line, which allows a lot of copy. For standard stationery, you may adjust your margins up to 1.75 inches to create an open, uncluttered appearance. Readers like wider margins because the page is more attractive and easier to read.
- After margins have been established, how much copy you can actually place on each line will be determined by the size of your type font.

Typical spacing for vertical alignment
- A short letter of fewer than 100 words typically has six to ten lines between the date and the inside address.
- A medium-length letter of 100 – 200 words typically has four or five lines between the date and the inside address.
- A long letter with more than 200 words typically has two or three lines between the date and the inside address.
- Extremely short letters of around 50 words can have wide left and right margins to compensate.

Adjusting letter alignment

Lengthening a short letter	Shortening a long letter
A short letter is about 7 – 8 lines of text including approximately 50 – 75 words.	A long letter is 25 lines of text or more using 200 words or more.
Increase the side margins.	Create smaller left and right margins.
Use a smaller size letterhead stationery.	Change to a standard stationery if you were using a smaller size.
Choose a larger type font that uses fewer characters per inch.	Choose a smaller type font, or one that allows more characters per inch. Adjusting the kerning (space between letters) and leading (the space between lines – rhymes with wedding) will allow more copy in the same space. Be very careful that you don't make the print so small that it becomes hard to read.
Lower the date line by as much as 4 – 6 inches. Leave 5 – 10 lines between the date and the inside address.	Reduce the space between the date and the inside address from the usual 5 lines to approximately 2 – 3 lines.
Leave up to 6 lines between the complimentary closing and the signature.	Reduce the space for the signature to 2 lines.
Lower reference initials, copy notations, and enclosure notations by 1 – 2 lines.	If you must have reference initials, place them on the same line as the writer's signature.

Letters of two pages or more

- Letterhead stationery is used on the first page only. All continuation pages use plain paper of similar quality with left and right margins that match the first page.
- The continuation page heading is typed on the first line below the one-inch margin at the top of the page. The heading information may be typed on either a single line or three separate lines.

1. Name of the recipient
2. Page number
3. Date

- Many word-processing programs can create a "header" that will automatically insert the continuation page details on each page.
- Text begins two lines below the continuation page heading.
- Never carry over the complimentary closing of a business letter to a continuation page. Adjust the spacing on the first page to allow the complete text to appear on a single page. If your closing must be on the second page, carry over at least two lines of the body of the letter to the second page.
- Normally leave at least a one-inch margin at the bottom of page 1, and make all other margins match the first page.
- If the page separation splits a paragraph, arrange it so that at least two typed lines remain on page 1 at the beginning of the paragraph and at least two lines of type appear at the end on page 2.
- Never hyphenate the last word on a page.

PREPARING PROFESSIONAL ENVELOPES

The easiest way to prepare an envelope is with word-processing software that has envelope templates. Then, you only have to select the envelope size and it will default to specific settings. You can also modify any of the menu items to suit your needs, or establish other specifications for a custom-size envelope if your printer will accept it. If you choose to type an envelope, the following guidelines will help.

Mailing address

- Always use single spacing and block each line at the left.

- Capitalize the first letter of every word in an address, except for *and*.

- Type the city, state, and ZIP Code on the last line, unless there is no room for the ZIP Code, in which case it may be placed directly below the last line, blocked on the left margin.

- Use the two-letter state code typed in capital letters.

- For No. 10 envelopes (the standard business size), type the mailing address four inches from the left edge and two inches from the top edge. For small envelopes, type the address two inches from the top edge and two and a half inches from the left edge.

Postal Service guidelines

U.S. Postal Service guidelines suggest that all-capital letters and no punctuation be used for mailing addresses. Created for the use of high-volume (bulk) mailers that generate addresses by computers or automated equipment, this style is preferred but not required for first-class mail. The traditional address style using upper and lower case as well as punctuation is more commonly seen on business letters, and Postal Service optical character readers (OCRs) can handle both styles. Writers who will be using mail-merge to generate envelopes from inside addresses on letters are more likely to use the traditional style.

Return address

- Use single-spaced lines, blocked on the left side.

- Place one item on each line: writer's name, company name, street address or P.O. box, and city/state/ZIP Code.

- Allow a minimum of one-half inch on the top and left margins.

Addressee notations

- Type any special directions three lines below the return address, one-half inch from the left edge.

- Start each key word with a capital letter, using bold print, italics, or underscoring. For special emphasis, notations such as PERSONAL or CONFIDENTIAL can be typed in all capitals.

- Other common notations are: Please Forward and Hold for Arrival.

If it is possible to cut a word out, always cut it out.

— George Orwell

INTRODUCTION LETTERS

New business associate
Hints for an ideal letter:

- Write in a positive and persuasive tone to stimulate the reader's interest.
- Introduce the new associate — name, position, and date of employment.
- Give background information on associate's education, experience, and previous employers.
- Reassure that the business relationship will continue.

Dear Preston:

I am happy to announce that, as of May 1, B&H Pharmaceuticals has a new division manager for the Southwestern Division — Jim McClusky. Jim will be the senior manager and will supervise all sales representatives responsible for calling on your organization. *— Introduction of associate*

As a fellow Longhorn, you will be pleased to know that Jim is a 1985 graduate of The University of Texas College of Pharmacy. He also has an MBA from UT and has ten years of experience in pharmaceutical sales and management. Previously, he was in a marketing position with Jackson Pharmaceuticals. *— Background information*

Jim will be calling you in the next two weeks to introduce himself and to schedule a luncheon meeting with you. Since your organization is a major purchaser of our products, we want to make sure our service continues to meet your expectations. *— Importance of relationship*

New form

Hints for an ideal letter:

- Begin by identifying the new form.
- Explain how the new form differs from the previous form.
- State the benefits of the new form.
- Close with contact information.

Dear Valued Customer:

In our commitment to improve our service to you, we have changed the format of our account statements.

On previous statements, your purchases were itemized by department, such as Functional Active, Petite Dresses, and Household Items. However, this description did not identify your specific purchase.

As you will notice on your current statement for July 1-31, your exact purchases are now identified by name — dress, shoes, toaster, camera, etc. We believe this format is easier to understand and will save you time when you are checking your statement.

If you have any questions about your transactions, please call our Customer Service Department at 1-800-345-1111. We appreciate your selecting our store for your purchases, and we look forward to serving you in the future.

Introduce change

Explain previous form

Describe change
Convey benefits

Offer assistance

New location

Hints for an ideal letter:

- Announce your new location, giving address and directions.
- Describe the products or services offered.
- Point out the benefits of the new location.
- Invite your reader to visit and offer an incentive.

Dear Ms. Temple:

Good News! Now Crocker's Office Supplies is just minutes away! We are ready to serve you at our newest location — 1219 West Sunset in Boca Raton, Florida (at the corner of West Sunset and Hollywood). *— Announcement of location*

Now the largest in our family, the West Sunset store carries more name-brand office supplies at discount prices than you will find anywhere else. Whether you are looking for business machines, furniture, writing instruments, or general office supplies, we will have it in stock or we will order it — at no extra cost to you. *— Benefits to reader*

For your printing needs, visit our Business Center and check the many services available — binding, copying, custom banners and signs, digital color copying, and design services. We can provide you with hundreds of options to enhance the image of your business cards, letterhead, envelopes, and announcements. *— Explanation of services*

Parking will be a snap when you drive into our multilevel covered parking lot. Once inside our store, any one of our office supply specialists will be ready to assist you. *— More benefits*

Drop by soon so we can say hello, show you around, and present you with a $15 certificate that you can apply toward your next purchase. We are proud to be your neighbor and hope you make Crocker's Office Supplies your first choice.

Visit us soon. *— Close with invitation*

HOW TO CREATE HIGH-IMPACT LETTERS, MEMOS, AND E-MAIL

New product/service
Hints for an ideal letter:

- Open with an attention-getting statement or question.
- Focus on benefits — not features.
- Identify how the product or service is unique.
- Create visual appeal — short paragraphs, short sentences, and bulleted lists.
- Make it easy to test or sample the product or service.
- Close by asking for a response.

Dear Melody C. Reiss:

  Would you like to access your account balance at any time? Or transfer funds between accounts? Or pay your bills online? Now you can — by using your personal computer and BANKING MADE EASY.

  BANKING MADE EASY is a revolutionary software program that allows you to do your banking online. All you need is a personal computer, and within minutes you can:

- Balance your checkbook
- Move funds from one account to another
- Find out your current checking, savings, and credit card balances
- Pay your monthly bills, such as car and mortgage

  Just think of it — no more waiting in lines or adjusting your schedule to bank hours. Instead, safe, secure, and simple banking from your home!

  And the best part of BANKING MADE EASY is it's free to our valued customers like you! That's right — no monthly fee, no hourly online fee, and no shipping and handling fee!

  All you need to do to begin using BANKING MADE EASY is to call 1-800-BANKEZE or mail the enclosed reply card. As soon as we hear from you, we'll send you your free BANKING MADE EASY software package.

  So don't delay — sign up today!

Attention-getting statement

Unique product

Bulleted list for visual appeal

Benefits

Benefits

Response information

Request

THANK-YOU LETTERS

Hospitality
Hints for an ideal letter:

- Open with thanks about the event or kindness.
- Be sincere and specific about what you appreciated.
- Close with a pleasant comment.

> In composing, as a general rule, run your pen through every other word you have written; you have no idea what vigor it will give your style.
>
> — Sydney Smith

Dear Ann:

From all of the staff, thank you for the appreciation dinner you hosted at the Headliners Club. The setting was wonderful, and the food was superb.

Trying to promote and maintain a positive attitude among the staff in these uncertain times is difficult. Your thoughtfulness and generosity definitely made us feel very special. It's a real boost to our morale to know our efforts are recognized.

We appreciate your thinking of us.

Gratitude about event

Sincere statement of appreciation

Pleasant comment

Assistance

Hints for an ideal letter:

- Convey a genuine tone throughout.
- Begin with a personal comment.
- Be specific in explaining how the reader assisted you.
- Close with a thank-you or an expression of gratitude.

Dear John:

　　Yesterday I presented my idea for a new marketing strategy for our home fitness gym to the management committee. It was a smashing success!

　　Your ideas and analysis of our competitors' products were extremely valuable. I couldn't have done the preparation without you.

　　Thank you so much for your help. I'll make sure the Vice President of Marketing knows how important your input was in developing the marketing strategy.

Personal comment

Assistance

Thank-you

Customer referral

Hints for an ideal letter:

- Open with a thank-you for the referral.
- Announce the outcome or expected outcome of the referral.
- Convey appreciation for the time invested.
- Close with a goodwill message.

Dear Harry:

Thank you for referring Vivian Harding to me. She called this afternoon to discuss her financial planning needs and to find out what services our firm offers.

After reviewing some basic issues over the telephone, I am confident that we can develop a financial plan that will meet her goals. We are scheduled to get together on September 15 to begin the planning process.

I know your plate is more than full at this time. To think about growing our business is more than generous of you.

I really appreciate the referral and the confidence you have in my firm.

Opening statement of thanks

Announcement of outcome

Expression of appreciation

Goodwill message

Gift

Hints for an ideal letter:

- Make it brief and sincere.
- Open by expressing appreciation.
- Describe a specific use of or benefit from the gift.
- End with a pleasant remark.

Dear Carrie:

The afghan depicting the "Images of Toledo" is a beauty! Thank you for surprising me with such a thoughtful gift.

The blanket creatively highlights the colorful history and pride of your city. My two favorite images are those of The University of Toledo and the Toledo Mud Hens — a slight contrast in choices. I suppose my enthusiasm for education and baseball led me to like those best.

The next time you visit, you will enjoy seeing the afghan prominently displayed in our lobby. It's a special addition!

Express appreciation

Personal comment

Special use
Pleasant remark

Invitation — accepting and declining
Hints for an ideal letter:

- Acknowledge the invitation.
- Graciously accept or decline the invitation.
- If declining, consider offering an explanation.
- End on a positive note.

Dear Dr. Gans:

Thank you for inviting me to participate in the "Medical Technology in the 21st Century" conference on August 20 – 23 in Washington, D.C. *— Acknowledgment*

I accept your invitation and look forward to participating in this prestigious event. As the timing nears, I will follow up with you about the conference logistics. *— Acceptance*

Dear Dr. Gans:

Your invitation to the "Medical Technology in the 21st Century" conference on August 20 – 23 in Washington, D.C. arrived today. *— Acknowledgment*

After checking my schedule, I realize I will be unable to attend your prestigious event. I will be representing my organization at a state association meeting in Boston during the same week. *— Decline*

Best wishes for a successful and productive conference. *— Positive note*

LETTERS OF REQUEST

Available product

Hints for an ideal letter:

- State your request.
- Give all relevant information — amounts, names, dates, etc.
- Explain your reason for the request.
- Give a deadline for the response.
- Make your request easy to answer — questionnaire; survey; self-addressed, stamped envelope.
- Close with appreciation.

Dear Mr. Hubbard:

I understand that your company manufactures custom sun screens for all types of automobiles. These sun screens fit inside the front windshield of the car and protect the interior from intense sun rays. — *Interest*

I am interested in obtaining information about sun screens for two automobiles:

1. 1994 Chevrolet Camaro
2. 1996 Buick Regal

— *Specific information*

I would appreciate your sending me a price quote detailing the cost of making a custom sun screen for each of these automobiles. — *Request*

Since summer is fast approaching, please send the estimate by June 15. I have enclosed a self-addressed, stamped envelope for your convenience. — *Deadline*

Thank you for your assistance. — *Appreciation*

HOW TO CREATE HIGH-IMPACT LETTERS, MEMOS, AND E-MAIL

Delivery requirement
Hints for an ideal letter:

- Open with a specific explanation of the information you need or the order you are placing.
- State the deadline.
- Ask the reader to respond to you; give contact information.
- Close by thanking the reader.

Dear E-Z-TEE Print Co.:

I am coordinating a walk-a-thon for the American Cancer Society on March 1 in Austin, Texas. — *Reason*

Since your company manufactures specially designed tee shirts, I am considering placing an order for 300 tee shirts. Specifically, I would need 200 white Extra Large and 100 white Large shirts made of 50 percent cotton and 50 percent polyester. The logo and wording (drawing enclosed) would be printed on the front of the shirts in red and blue. — *Specific details*

I would need the order delivered by February 15 to allow time for distributing the shirts to our members. Please let me know by return mail whether you can guarantee delivery on or before this date. If you would prefer calling me directly, you can reach me Monday through Friday from 8 a.m. to 5 p.m. at 512-325-6000. — *Deadline / Request*

Thank you for letting me know whether the date of February 15 will fit your manufacturing schedule. — *Appreciation*

HOW TO CREATE HIGH-IMPACT LETTERS, MEMOS, AND E-MAIL

"Yes" response to a request
Hints for an ideal letter:

- Thank the reader for the request.
- Explain what you can do.
- Conclude by offering future assistance or expressing appreciation.

> The most valuable of all talents is that of never using two words when one will do.
>
> — Thomas Jefferson

Dear Mr. Kimball:

Thank you for your letter requesting a copy of the Azle Computer Corp. Quarterly Shareowners Report for the quarter ended March 31.

Thank-you

We are enclosing the quarterly report as well as a copy of our annual report. You will find a summary of the company's financial performance and highlights of major acquisitions and transactions. You will note that Azle has experienced a record-breaking year.

Action taken

If you would be interested in a transcript of the annual meeting or an audiotape of the chairman's message, please let us know. Just call Azle Shareowner Services toll free at 1-800-123-4567.

Future assistance

We appreciate your interest and support of our organization.

Appreciation

"No" response to a request
Hints for an ideal letter:

- Open on a positive note.
- Give a reason(s) for the refusal.
- Give the actual refusal.
- If possible, offer alternatives.
- Be tactful and considerate throughout the letter.

Dear Ms. VanLandingham:

Thank you for informing us about the work you are doing for disabled veterans.

At the start of each year, our finance committee determines the funds to be allocated for civic and charitable donations. As requests are received, we consider each organization and its respective cause. Typically there are more requests received than funds available.

Since we have already committed our 19XX funds for corporate giving, we are unable to contribute to your program this year. However, please consider resubmitting your proposal by December 1 for our next fiscal year. In early January, our finance committee once again will meet to evaluate all requests for corporate contributions.

We admire the commendable work you are doing for a most deserving group.

Positive opening

Reason for refusal

Refusal
Alternative

Tactful and sincere close

ANNOUNCEMENT LETTERS

New address
Hints for an ideal letter:

- Announce the move.
- Give the new address and telephone number.
- Describe the benefits of the move.
- Close with an invitation to call or visit the new location.

Dear Mr. Powers:

We are moving!

Effective August 6, 19XX, Jackson, Houston, and Crockett, P.C. will be located in downtown San Antonio. Our new address will be a familiar one:

> The Boone Building
> 400 Travis Street, Suite 300
> San Antonio, TX 78207
> 210/321-6400
> 210/321-6440 (Fax)

Why are we moving? For two reasons.

1. We want to locate our firm in the area where 70 percent of our clients reside. By bringing our firm closer to you, we will be able to serve you more effectively.

2. Because of an increasing staff, we have an immediate need to expand our office space.

The enclosed map highlights our new location. The ten-story secured parking garage adjacent to our building will provide you with adequate parking at no cost to you.

To celebrate our move, we are hosting a "Welcome" reception from 5 p.m. to 8 p.m. on August 15. We hope you will have the opportunity to attend, enjoy hors d'oeuvres and refreshments, and meet the members of our firm.

Announcement

New address and telephone number

Benefits of move

Invitation to visit

New business

Hints for an ideal letter:

- Introduce yourself and your business.
- State the location and telephone number.
- Describe the products or services you offer.
- Explain your competitive advantage.
- Follow up with a telephone call or extend an invitation to visit or call.

Dear Ms. Jacobsen:

Alex Grosby and Lawrence Klein are pleased to announce their new business venture — GROSBY KLEIN & CO. — accountants and consultants.

GROSBY KLEIN & COMPANY
2700 West Scofield Drive
Wilton, CT 06897
203/834-1234

GROSBY KLEIN & COMPANY provides accounting and consulting services for growth-oriented businesses. With over 30 years of experience, we offer a comprehensive range of accounting, auditing, tax, litigation support, and consulting services tailored to fit your needs. Our specialized services are designed to help our clients solve business challenges and respond rapidly to ever-changing business environments.

What sets us apart from other accounting and consulting firms is our commitment to personal service. Every client relationship is treated with special personal attention. From the beginning, you will have access to either one of the firm principals — Alex Grosby or Lawrence Klein. You will then be assigned to a CPA who specializes in your particular business or profession. During all phases of your project, your work will be supervised and reviewed by either principal.

We would like the opportunity to tell you more about our services and show you our commitment to offering an exceptional level of service. We will call you in the next week to introduce ourselves.

Introduction of business

Description of services or products

Competitive advantage

Follow-up

Price increase

Hints for an ideal letter:

- Use a positive tone.
- Announce the price increase.
- Explain the reasons for the increase.
- Emphasize the benefits of your product or service.
- Close with a goodwill message.

> Anything written to please the author is worthless.
>
> — Blaise Pascal

Dear Subscriber:

For the last three years, the subscription rate for the Georgetown Chronicle has remained constant. Our number one objective has been to provide quality journalism to our readers at a reasonable price. *— Positive tone*

However, rising paper and labor costs have forced us to reevaluate our monthly subscription rate. Effective March 1, our monthly rate will increase from $12.50 to $13.50. *— Reasons / Announcement*

This slight increase will allow us to continue publishing an award-winning newspaper — one that is read throughout Central Missouri. In addition, we will be able to maintain our consistently reliable home delivery service. *— Benefits*

We appreciate having you as a reader, and we are grateful for your continuing support of our newspaper. If you have questions, please call us at 1-800-777-7777. *— Goodwill*

SALES LETTERS

Advertising

Hints for an ideal letter:

- Stimulate interest from the start.
- Introduce the advertising medium.
- Emphasize benefits to capture the reader's attention.
- Close by encouraging immediate action.

Dear Attorney:

Are you interested in expanding your client base and generating more income? If so, the Tri-State Medical Journal is just the right advertising publication for your firm.

Just look at the exposure you will receive. Our monthly journal is mailed to 90 percent of the physicians in New York, New Jersey, and Pennsylvania. That's an incredible number of readers you can reach every 30 days!

What better publication is there to promote your legal services? Think of it. Physicians are all too familiar with the word "malpractice" these days. More than ever before, they are in dire need of top-notch legal representation. But often they are uncertain where to turn for help. Why not invite them to turn to you?

So how can you take advantage of this outstanding marketing opportunity? By sending us a camera-ready copy of a one-quarter, one-half, or full-page advertisement. The enclosed rate sheet describes our advertising fees and easy-to-follow guidelines for submitting copy.

We encourage you to call us at 1-800-MEDICAL to discuss your advertising program. We are ready to introduce you to thousands of physicians who can benefit from professional legal representation.

Let us hear from you soon!

Attention-getting opener
Introduction
Benefits

Reason

Enclosure

Contact information

Products/programs/services

Hints for an ideal letter:

- Capture the reader's attention in the first sentence.
- Stimulate interest by using descriptive words (imagery).
- Emphasize benefits — not just features.
- Create visual appeal with short paragraphs, short sentences, and short words.
- Mention the cost and give details about how to obtain the product, program, or service.
- Encourage the reader to take immediate action, and make it easy for the reader to respond.

Dear Mr. Pappadeaux:

Tired. Out of shape. Flabby. Overweight. Is that how you feel and look? — *Descriptive words to capture attention*

Energetic. Firm. Muscular. Trim. Isn't that how you'd rather feel and look?

You can! We at Good Health Fitness Center are ready to design a fitness program to help you achieve your desired weight. And at an incredibly low introductory price of $15/week! — *Cost*

Now is the time to shed those pounds you've been carrying around! Discover how easy it is with our state-of-the-art facility offering the latest in weight machines, treadmills, bicycles, and free weights. And for the outdoor enthusiast, jog your way to good health on our figure-eight running track or swim countless laps in our beautiful Olympic-size swimming pool. Plus, we're open seven days a week from 6 a.m. to 10 p.m. to accommodate you and your schedule. — *Benefits*

We urge you to call today to take advantage of our special "Get Ready for Summer" offer. Enroll by April 10 and receive a complimentary GOOD HEALTH FITNESS CENTER workout shirt. And then for an additional $7.50/week, the whole family can enjoy the privilege of exercising in a "FOR MEMBERS ONLY" fitness center. — *Incentive*

Just call us at 348-6377 (FITNESS) to schedule an appointment with one of our professional trainers. In no time at all, we'll have you on the road to fitness and good health. — *Request for action*

Follow-up

Hints for an ideal letter:

- Begin by thanking the reader for the opportunity to talk or meet with you.
- Summarize the benefits and features of your product, service, or program.
- End with a statement of action.

Dear Ms. Chatelle:

Thank you for making the time to meet with me on Tuesday to discuss your current training needs. I'm delighted Toni Gerthoffer arranged for us to get together.

Your commitment to your staff members' professional development is commendable. In thinking more about a program to strengthen their writing skills, I am enclosing a description of our one-day "Effective Business Writing" workshop. This practical, skill-building seminar will help your staff members to:

- Overcome any fear of writing and build their confidence
- Write more clearly and persuasively
- Turn around writing projects faster and with less supervision on your part
- Minimize costly communication errors
- Project a polished, service-minded image to your clients
- Take on increasingly difficult assignments, freeing up your time for other responsibilities

As you'll notice, the program is divided into four sections representing the four phases of the writing process — prewriting, writing, editing, and rewriting. Each section is supported by guidelines, examples, and exercises. Your staff members will be able to practice immediately what they're learning.

When you've had a chance to review the program outline, I will call you to discuss scheduling and customizing. I look forward to talking with you the week of October 20.

Thank-you

Benefits

Features

Action step

ORDERS

Confirming a delivery
Hints for an ideal letter:

- Respond as soon as the order is received.
- Reconfirm the delivery date.
- Repeat the specific details of the order — quantity, description of merchandise, and cost.
- Thank the customer.

Dear Mr. Roumbanis:

Thank you for the order you placed with us on January 17. We are pleased to confirm your delivery date of February 1 for the following items: *— Confirmation of delivery date*

- 3 Burke Ergonomic Fully Adjustable Chairs
     Blue/Gray – $149.99 each

- 2 Conan Executive Chairs
     Blue/Gray – $239.99 each   *— Specific details of order*

- 4 Wainwright Typist Chairs
     Midnight Blue – $69.99 each

If you have any questions, just call our Customer Service Department at 1-800-FOR HELP Monday through Friday from 8 a.m. to 5 p.m. Any of our customer service representatives will be ready to assist you. To save you time, please have your Confirmation Number 173836 handy.

We appreciate your business and look forward to serving you again. *— Appreciative close*

HOW TO CREATE HIGH-IMPACT LETTERS, MEMOS, AND E-MAIL

I never understand anything until I have written about it.

— E. M. Forster

Insufficient information

Hints for an ideal letter:

- Acknowledge that you have received the order.
- Ask for the additional information.
- Give a brief explanation.
- End on a positive note.

Dear Ms. Graham:

We need your help!

We are ready to ship your order for the Leadership Assessment Surveys and Personality Profile Indicators. However, the shipping address you provided us is a post office box instead of a street address.

Our contracted delivery service, Expedite Express, is unable to deliver orders to a post office box. Instead, the carrier needs a specific street address to guarantee delivery.

Please call our Order Department at 1-800-EXPRESS so we can change your address. Once we hear from you, we will ship your order within 24 hours.

Thank you for calling us.

Acknowledgment of order

Brief explanation

Request for additional information

Positive close

Insufficient information (cont.)

Dear Ms. Graham:

Your Leadership Assessment Surveys and Personality Profile Indicators are ready to be shipped to you as soon as we receive your payment.

Just let us know your preferred payment method by completing the following information:

☐ Check or Money Order
☐ C.O.D.
☐ Credit Card

_____
Credit Card Number

_____
Expiration Date

_____
Signature

If calling us would be more convenient, you can reach us at 1-800-EXPRESS. Or you can fax the information to 1-987-654-3210. We appreciate your understanding that all orders must be prepaid.

Thank you for the opportunity to serve you.

Acknowledgment of order

Request for additional information

Brief explanation

Positive close

Order cancellation

Hints for an ideal letter:

- Identify the specific order — item number, quantity, description of merchandise, and cost.
- Cancel the order.
- Ask for a refund or a credit.
- Request a confirmation of the cancellation.

Attn: Order Department

On September 15 we ordered the following items:

ITEM #	QUANTITY	DESCRIPTION	COST
841-156	12	Ballpoint Pens, Chrome	$14.99
257-094	12	Ballpoint Pen Refills	2.99
934-278	12	Mechanical Pencils	3.99
512-318	24	Mechanical Pencil Leads	.99
367-114	3	Electric Pencil Sharpeners	17.99

We need to cancel our order.

These items were charged to Corporate Account #AGS-51715. Please credit our account for the total amount. Also, we would appreciate your sending us a confirmation of this cancellation for our records.

Thank you for your assistance.

Identification of order

Cancellation

Request for credit and confirmation

Order change

Hints for an ideal letter:

- Identify full details of your initial order.
- State the changes you need to make.
- Request a written confirmation.

Attn: Institute for Professional Development

Re: "Project Management" Seminar
       Program #67348
       May 31 – San Antonio, Texas

Specific details

One of our associates, Mr. Jason Dougherty, is scheduled to attend your "Project Management" seminar on May 31 in San Antonio, Texas. Because of a scheduling conflict, he is unable to participate in that program. We would like to substitute another associate, Ms. Siri Sumbera, in his place. Please transfer the $149 enrollment fee for Mr. Dougherty to cover Ms. Sumbera's registration.

Change #1

We also would like to enroll two additional associates in your May 31 program — Mr. Michael Castillo and Ms. Sonja Mann. Our check for $298 is enclosed to cover these two additional registrations.

Change #2

Please send us written confirmations for these three registrations, noting the seminar title, date, time, location, and customer number.

Confirmation request

Thank you for making these changes.

Attn: Samuelson's Stationery Supplies

We are interested in ordering the following greeting cards from your 19XX Holiday Catalog:

ITEM #	QUANTITY	DESCRIPTION	COST
#G5650	50	Western Santa and Reindeer	$63.95
#G7843	50	Holly Wreath	49.95
#G1892	50	Hanukkah Wishes	55.95
#G2539	50	World at Peace	59.95

Please charge these greeting cards to our corporate credit card #5643-292-881-909 and deliver to the attention of:

> Mr. Carl Moore
> M.H. Spectrum and Associates
> 6804 Beauford Drive
> San Francisco, CA 94122

To verify you have received this order, please send us a written confirmation. Also, we would appreciate knowing when we can expect delivery of the greeting cards.

Thank you.

Charging an order
Hints for an ideal letter:

- Identify the specific details of the order — item number, quantity, description of merchandise, and cost.
- Request the order be charged to a credit card or account number.
- Give the shipping address.
- Ask for a written confirmation and an estimated delivery date.

Identification of order

Request to charge order

Shipping address

Request for confirmation and delivery date

Order confirmation

Hints for an ideal letter:

- Confirm the order as soon as you receive it.
- Repeat specific details of the order — quantity, item, model number, price, delivery date, carrier, and billing information.
- Thank the customer.

Dear Ms. Dodson:

As a follow-up to your telephone order on July 22, we would like to confirm the following items:

    1 TOPCO Computer Model #ZKS52 with standard software package – $1499.00

    1 WHITNEY Plain Paper Fax Machine Model #570M – $499.99

    1 CARDINAL Copier Model #3666 – $699.00

We expect these items to be shipped on July 30 by Rapid Delivery System and to arrive no later than August 10. As you requested, the entire order, including shipping and handling fees, will be charged to your corporate account — #TDA46397.

If you have a question about your order, please call us at our 24-hour toll-free number — 1-800-WESERVE. We are ready to help you at any time.

Thank you for being such a valued customer. We certainly appreciate your business.

Order confirmation

Specific details

Confirmation of delivery and payment

Offer to help

Thank-you

APOLOGY LETTERS

Delay

Hints for an ideal letter:

- Make sure your tone is warm and sincere.
- Be specific about explanations offered.
- Avoid a tone that appears to make excuses.
- Tell your customer exactly when the desired item will be available.
- Offer your help if needed.

Dear Ms. Hansen:

Thank you for writing to our Customer Service Department to tell us about the delay in receiving your magazine subscription. I understand that you were told your issues would begin arriving at your house October 1. We know how important it is to you to receive your magazine in a timely fashion.

After researching your account, we have learned that a data-entry error triggered your subscription to begin December 1, rather than October 1. You will receive your first issue approximately December 3 and the normal subscription will continue through November 1 of next year. We do apologize for the delay in receiving your magazine and would like to offer you three complimentary issues. Your subscription will now run through February 1, 19xx.

We know you will enjoy the many exciting features and comprehensive information our magazine offers you. If you have any additional questions, please call me directly at xxx-xxxx.

Sincere tone

Specific explanation
When available
Apology, not excuse

Offer to help

Misunderstanding

Hints for an ideal letter:

- Explain briefly how the mistake/misunderstanding occurred.
- Acknowledge that it may have inconvenienced the reader.
- Discuss any actions you have taken to guarantee that the mistake/misunderstanding does not happen again.
- Be sincere and open.
- Discuss any follow-up needed at this point.

Dear Erik:

I realized this morning that the new directory of Missouri cities and towns that you needed for your meeting yesterday had not been sent last week as promised. The note to my administrative assistant had been inadvertently clipped to a folder that had been set aside, and it was just today that we saw it during a priorities review. — *Explain mistake*

Your meeting participants would have benefited from the demographic data, and I suspect that it may have been somewhat embarrassing for you to not have had it available. — *Acknowledge inconvenience*
Please know that I apologize for any inconvenience that this may have caused you. — *Apology*

In the future, I will forward the request to my assistant immediately at the end of the phone call, as well as making a note in my calendar to check that any requested information has been mailed. — *Future actions*

I've enclosed your directory, and if you need any additional reference material, please call me directly at xxx-xxxx. I'll promise right now that your request will always have a top priority with me! — *Follow-up / Sincere closing*

Accepting partial responsibility

What's wrong with this letter:

- Critical tone
- Condescending
- Reluctant assistance
- Negative words

WRONG WAY

Dear Ms. Reynolds:

We received the letter you sent regarding the error in the résumé that our office prepared and printed for you. We at PROFESSIONAL IMAGES do take pride in the work we do for our clients because we know how important it is to make a good impression on a potential employer.

However, we cannot control mistakes that you may make in the information you provide us, or errors that you do not find when you check the final draft. Our advertisements clearly state that any errors that you do not correct will be your responsibility.

After speaking with my typesetter and proofreader, I understand that you were given an opportunity to correct the final draft before it was printed. Their log notes show that you did a telephone approval on April 21 and did not carefully review the draft in person. We certainly would have faxed you a copy if you weren't able to come to our office, but it was up to you to take the final responsibility for the finished product.

While we can fully understand your distress that the incorrect résumé was mailed to the Anderson & Baines office along with your cover letter, at this point there is not much that can be done. Although we are very clear about checking final drafts, and feel that this situation is your responsibility, we would be willing to print new résumés at no cost to you.

In the future, please make sure that you see a copy of the final draft before something is printed.

Condescending

Negative

Critical

Reluctant assistance

HOW TO CREATE HIGH-IMPACT LETTERS, MEMOS, AND E-MAIL

Accepting partial responsibility

Hints for an ideal letter:

- Validate a customer or client's concern, even if you are not fully responsible for the problem.
- Offer your unique perspective about the circumstances.
- Maintain an interested rather than cold or detached tone.
- Be careful about admitting liability in case it may affect future actions your customer may take.
- Emphasize anything that you can do to alleviate the situation.
- Guarantee that the reader will feel that the customer relationship and goodwill are important to you.

RIGHT WAY

Dear Ms. Reynolds:

Thank you for letting me know of the concern you had about an error in the résumé that our office prepared and printed for you. We at PROFESSIONAL IMAGES pride ourselves on the impression that we help you create with prospective employers, and appreciate how very important this is to you!

After speaking with my typesetter and proofreader, I understand that you were given an opportunity to correct the final draft before it was printed. Their log notes show that you did a telephone approval on April 21 and did not have a chance to see that copy. It is most likely that the mistake would have been discovered at that "final draft review" before your résumé was printed.

While we can fully understand your distress that the incorrect résumé was mailed to the Anderson & Baines office along with your cover letter, at this point the best option is to print new résumés at no cost to you. Please make sure that you see a copy of the final draft before we print it. Our goal is to help you look terrific during your job search, and we'll do whatever we can to make that happen!

Sincere tone

Validation

Unique perspective

No liability

Empathy

Future action

Goodwill

Company policy doesn't allow the customer's request
What's wrong with this letter:

- Assumes the customer is wrong
- Uses abrupt language for the refusal
- Has mild sarcasm

WRONG WAY

Dear Ms. Proctor:

We regret the problems you have had with two of the microwaves in the employee breakroom. It sounds like everyone is trying to have lunch at about the same time, so the ovens have probably been overworked and abused.

I have checked the records of your equipment purchase and found that your warranty on the microwaves expired July 31. Since it is now September 6, we will be unable to repair your ovens at our expense as you requested. At this point, however, you have two choices: 1) we can repair the ovens for the usual repair fee, or 2) we can offer you an extended warranty plan at a very reasonable cost that will cover those repairs and provide you further protection in the future. We suggest that you consider such a warranty, since your company tends to have a lot of wear and tear on the equipment.

The enclosed pamphlet reviews the highlights of the warranty and should answer most of your questions. I would be glad to set you up on the extended plan and get your microwaves scheduled for immediate service.

Assume customer is wrong

Abrupt language

Condescending attitude

Mild sarcasm

HOW TO CREATE HIGH-IMPACT LETTERS, MEMOS, AND E-MAIL

Company policy doesn't allow the customer's request
Hints for an ideal letter:

- Acknowledge that the customer has a legitimate issue.
- Explain concisely what your policy does and does not allow.
- State tactfully what actions can occur now.
- Keep your tone light or neutral, not severe.
- Assume that once your customer understands the facts of the situation, your business relationship will continue.

RIGHT WAY

Dear Ms. Proctor:

    We appreciate your letting us hear about the problems you have had with two of the microwaves in the employee breakroom. It must be frustrating trying to get your meals heated when everyone has lunch at approximately the same time. We know you will want to get this resolved as quickly as possible.

    I have checked the records of your equipment purchase and found that your warranty on the microwaves was in force until July 31. Murphy's law seems to have struck again! Since it is now September 6, we will be unable to repair your ovens at our expense as you requested. However, we can offer you an extended warranty plan at a very reasonable cost that will cover all repairs now and offer you solid protection in the future.

    The enclosed pamphlet reviews the highlights of the warranty and should answer most of your questions. I would be delighted to set you up on the extended plan and get your microwaves scheduled for immediate repair.

    I know the employees will be very happy to get their ovens back in the breakroom.

Acknowledgment

Light tone

Explanation

What happens now

Continuing relationship

Positive ending

Customer received poor service
Hints for an ideal letter:

- Open with a warm or appreciative comment.
- Open with an apology as an alternative.
- Briefly explain the reasons for the poor service.
- State action steps that will correct the problem.
- Close with an expression of goodwill.

Dear Mr. Marcus:

We certainly appreciate the time you took to let us know about the difficulty you had obtaining the forms you needed to file your variance. Our customer service lobby tries very hard to minimize the waiting time for our clients, and employees do realize that people are in a hurry when they come in. You're right when you say that the quality of service provided is the most important issue for government offices today. — *Warmth*

I have researched the reasons for the delay that you experienced and discovered that we had two of our employees out of work with the flu the day you visited. The waiting time indeed was about 20 minutes longer than normal. I do apologize for the inconvenience. — *Explanation / Apology*

Your ideas for improved service were excellent, and I received quite a positive reaction to the self-service racks from the managers. We expect to be able to implement that within 60 days. In addition, we are performing some new cross-training that will allow us to bring employees from other departments to fill in when others are sick. We believe that these new efforts will offer more effective service even during busy periods. — *Corrective steps*

Thank you for your suggestions and know that we look forward to the opportunity to have you visit our office again. You'll be pleased to see the new look! — *Goodwill*

PROPOSALS

Contract proposal
Hints for an ideal letter:
- State specific deliverables.
- State deadlines or due dates.
- Specify ownership of finished products, if necessary.
- State requirements, such as work that must be all original.
- Request formal signatures.
- Request Social Security/Taxpayer Identification Number to save time for issuance of purchase orders, checks, etc.

Dear Mr. Sanborn:

New Horizons Airline requests that you prepare the following materials for its sole use:

Description of Work: New Employee Orientation Manual
Deadline: April 1, 19xx

New Horizons agrees to pay you $2,000 upon receipt of the finished manual. You understand that this product is a "work made for hire" and New Horizons owns all rights to the manual in the name of either New Horizons or its parent company, Northern Airlines. You will warrant that this work has not been in the public domain or previously created, and that the work will be free of unauthorized excerpting from other sources. You further understand that New Horizons will have the privilege of referring to you in promotional material.

Please indicate your acceptance of this agreement by completing the form below and returning it to us no later than December 1.

For New Horizon Airlines and Northern Airlines Inc.
Name _____
Title _____
Date _____
TO: New Horizon Airlines/Northern Airlines Inc.

I agree to perform the above "work for hire" according to the terms and conditions stated by the declared deadline.

Signature _____
Company name _____
Date _____
Social Security Number or TIN _____
(Required by I.R.S. regulations)

Specific deliverable due date
Payment

Ownership
Originality

Deadline

Signature

Legal requirements

Decision not yet made

Hints for an ideal letter:

- Use straightforward, nonevasive language.
- Offer concise explanations where possible.
- Use a neutral tone.
- State "next step" procedures where applicable.
- Offer a resource for questions and follow-up.

Dear Mr. Bowen:

We know that you have been eager to hear of our decision on the purchase of the new printers for our Accounting and Billing Department. This letter will inform you of a brief delay in our evaluation process.

The Accounting and Billing Department experienced a re-organization within the last 30 days. All of our pending equipment purchases have been postponed until we determine the new departmental structure and purchasing allowances. We expect that this will take an additional 60 days, and at that time we will choose the vendor for our new printers.

At the time of the postponement, your company was part of the final list from which the vendor will be chosen. We will notify you by mail no later than February 15 if your company is awarded the contract.

Thank you for your patience. You may call me directly at xxx-xxxx if you have further questions or need additional information.

Straightforward language

Explanation

Neutral tone
Next step

Resource

Request for proposal

Hints for an ideal letter:

- Be specific about what you need from the vendor.
- State quantities.
- State delivery dates.
- Identify where and to whom the bid will be submitted.
- If payment terms will influence your decision, request that these be included.

Dear Sales Manager:

Investco Ltd. is designing a new sales training center and requests your proposal for the following equipment:

1.) 4 10x10 projection screens
2.) 2 8x8 projection screens
3.) 6 flipchart stands
4.) 4 gross permanent marking pens
5.) 6 overhead projectors
6.) 6 50-ft. extension cords
7.) 50 8-ft. tables
8.) 300 padded chairs

Delivery will be taken on or after July 1.

Please send your cost proposal to Dan Jenkins, Training Director, Investco Ltd., 2310 Highway 114, Omaha, NE 68130.

Your bid, including payment terms and/or credit options, is due no later than Friday, May 1.

Specific details

Quantities

Delivery date

Submission information

Payment terms

Proposal accepted

Hints for an ideal letter:

- Congratulate the successful bidder.
- State an outstanding element of the proposal, if applicable.
- State the next action steps.
- Express an expectation of success, if applicable.

Dear Ms. Marshall:

On behalf of Burton Advertising Inc., I am pleased to inform you that your proposal for redecoration of our corporate offices has been accepted. As a management team, we were extremely impressed with your bold and innovative use of color and fabrics. The portfolio documentation was outstanding, and your previous clients raved about the entire experience of working with you.

We are eager to begin our "makeover," and know that both our clients and our employees will be excited about the changes. Let's set a date for our project design meeting. Will June 10 work for you? I have set aside the entire day to create our action plan and examine initial samples from you. It will get us on the right road, and you can "tweak" the plan after the meeting. I would like to present our finalized design plan to the executives at their June 20 meeting.

I know that together we will invent an exciting new look for Burton that will be recognized by our colleagues as future oriented and original. See you on the 10th!

PS: Be sure to bring the art portfolio ... I am really leaning toward those Warhol prints for the conference room!

Congratulations

Special proposal element

Action steps

Expectation of success

Proposal rejected

Hints for an ideal letter:

- Make an appreciative comment about the bid.

- State specifically why the proposal wasn't accepted. (This will avoid "Why weren't we selected?" questions later.)

- Leave the door open for a possible future bid. (You may need this vendor's product or service someday.)

> No one can write decently who is distrustful of the reader's intelligence, or whose attitude is patronizing.
>
> – E. B. White

Dear Mr. Johannson:

   We appreciate the very professional presentation you made to our managers and staff last Thursday. We can certainly see why Excell Construction has such a positive reputation as a quality builder in this community. One of the drawbacks of your proposal is the exclusive use of wood-frame construction. After much discussion, the management team has decided upon the use of insulated concrete forms.

   We see many advantages in using the insulated forms. The energy savings (30 percent to 80 percent for most occupants) are outstanding, and the safety is reassuring since the building is fire and wind-resistant as well as bulletproof. A unique feature of concrete is the sound-deadening that creates a quieter and more productive work area. We have therefore decided to go with Hemsley Brothers, who gave us an excellent quote on the use of concrete. Their building process will create exactly the office addition that we want.

   We will retain your company on our bid list, and look forward to hearing from you when future projects are quoted.

Appreciative comment

Specific reason for declining

Explanation for successful bid

Open door

EMPLOYMENT LETTERS

Application
What's wrong with this letter:

- Grammatical errors
- Typos
- Misspellings

WRONG WAY

To the Attention of the Hireing Manger:

Please consider my application for the position of specialist in the hunan resources department as advertised in the Arzona Republic on Sunday, April 17.

My education, skills, and experience, which is detailed in the enclosed résumé, should qualify me for this postion. I will graduate from ASU next month with a Bachelor of Science degree in business administration. My course of study included classes in human resources development, wage and salary administration, and personnel research and measurement. All of these gives me a unique insight into the concerns the human resources staff persons today must face.

This understanding has been complimented by my practical experience in retailing. Having worked as both a salesperson in women's clothing at Dillard's, and an evening housewares manager at Albertson's, I have firsthand knowledge of human resources concerns. This combination of educational background and work experience should, I believe, makes me an asset to your company.

May I have an opportunity to interview for the specialist's job? I will call your office on Monday, April 25, to arrange a mutually convienient time. Please telephone me at 602-xxx-xxxx if you require any additional information.

Misspellings

Typos

Grammatical errors

Application

Hints for an ideal letter:

- Highlight key elements of your résumé without just repeating what it says.
- If you attended an interview, thank the reader for taking the time to meet with you.
- State that you do want the job.
- State why you believe you are the best candidate for the position.

RIGHT WAY

To the Attention of the Hiring Manager:

Please consider my application for the position of specialist in the human resources department as advertised in the Arizona Republic on Sunday, April 17.

My education, skills, and experience, which are detailed in the enclosed résumé, should qualify me for this position. I will graduate from ASU next month with a Bachelor of Science degree in business administration. My course of study included classes in human resources development, wage and salary administration, and personnel research and measurement. All of these gave me a unique insight into the concerns the human resources staff person today must face.

This understanding has been complemented by my practical experience in retailing. Having worked as both a salesperson in women's clothing at Dillard's and an evening housewares manager at Albertson's, I have firsthand knowledge of human resources concerns. This combination of educational background and work experience should, I believe, make me an asset to your company.

May I have an opportunity to interview for the specialist's job? I will call your office on Monday, April 25, to arrange a mutually convenient time. Please telephone me at 602-xxx-xxxx if you require any additional information.

Do want job

Résumé highlights

Best candidate

Action steps

Job query

Hints for an ideal letter:

- State specific request for job information.
- Inquire about job details (if needed).
- Offer to send a résumé or other credentials.
- Provide just a few relevant details.
- Ask for a follow-up.

Dear Ms. Hill:

My friend Krista Hedstrom, who works for Allied Systems, said that several recent job postings will now be advertised in the local newspaper after a lengthy internal search. I have considered applying for the jobs that seem to require my skills and experience but would find some additional details helpful.

While I'm not seeking a specific position at this time, I would like to request about 30 minutes of your time for an informational interview. I would like to see if my background is appropriate for such positions as: administrative assistant, senior secretary, or senior clerk. I am particularly interested to learn whether these jobs require spreadsheet experience as well as regular word processing. This would help me determine if it would be a good idea to apply for the advertised positions.

I'll be calling you soon to check on your availability for a brief meeting. Krista has said so many positive things about the company that it would be a privilege to be able to get your perspective on whether it would be a good match for my skills. Thank you.

Ask for job information

State specific request

Inquire about job details

Follow-up request

Recommendation

Hints for an ideal letter:

- State personal knowledge of or experience with the person you are recommending.
- Offer a few complimentary details.
- Don't sound gushy or overemotional.
- Provide a telephone number where the reader may contact you with questions.

To the Attention of the Hiring Representative:

Subject: Recommendation for Susan Albright

I am pleased to recommend Susan Albright to you as a potential employee. I have worked with Susan as a peer for almost eight years in the dental field and know for a fact that she is a very competent hygienist. Her people skills are also terrific — she has built a loyal following in our office the last several years. *— Personal knowledge of subject*

Everyone who works with Susan as a colleague or comes to her as a patient comments on how positive her attitude always is. I have never seen her in a bad mood, even on days that have been incredibly stressful. She maintains a calm demeanor, always smiles, and follows up with every patient consistently. *— Complimentary details*

I have enjoyed tremendously my association with Susan, and know that she would bring those same skills and qualities to any office she works in. Susan would not have left this office except for the out-of-state transfer of her husband, so Minnesota's loss is Florida's gain … *— Light tone*

Please call me for any additional information or questions that you may have. I would be delighted to discuss Susan further!

Follow-up letter
Hints for an ideal letter:

- Refer to the previous actions, discussions, interview, or interaction.
- State the reason for this letter.
- Make your request.
- Keep it short! Don't be aggressive or pushy.

Dear Ms. Carter-Collins:

Thank you for the postcard that acknowledged the arrival of my résumé and application. I'm sure that you must have received many letters because of the excellent reputation the Office of Environmental Quality has locally. Everyone wants to be part of a department that is doing cutting-edge technological breakthroughs. — *Previous actions*

I am curious about the next stage of the hiring process. I would like to know if interviews will be set up for a selected group of applicants, if there is a testing process, if letters of recommendation should be gathered at this point, and within what time frame these actions will take place. — *Reason for this letter*

May I ask that you give me a brief phone call to provide the additional information? I am also willing to call your office if there is someone else I should speak to. — *Request* Thanks very much for your time and attention, and I look forward to hearing from you soon. — *Appreciation*

Accepting a job offer
Hints for an ideal letter:

- Write an appreciation statement about receiving the offer.
- Formally state your acceptance of the offer.
- If salary negotiations have been part of your interview process, write the amount you have agreed upon.
- Offer a complimentary comment about why you are excited about joining the organization.
- If follow-up actions exist, mention exactly when you will call to finalize details.

Dear Mr. Winfield:

    Thank you for your offer to become part of the Quality Assurance Team at Henneger-Brockton Labs. The salary of $42,000 with the standard benefits package and a $5,000 tuition bank for advanced study is acceptable to me.

    The dedicated and professional team that I met during the interviewing procedure is a group that I am proud to join. I know that my skills and background will mesh nicely with theirs, and I will make a contribution to the Quality Improvement Process at H-B.

    We discussed a potential starting date of July 15, and I will call you next Monday to confirm that and see if any other paperwork must be completed prior to the 15th.

    Alternate paragraph if starting date is not co
We discussed a potential starting date of July 15, but I have a keynote speaking engagement at the International Quality Assurance Conference on July 17 in Atlanta. Is there any problem with moving the date ahead to July 20, since that is a Monday?

    I am looking forward to meeting with you again soon.

Appreciation
Salary
Formal acceptance

Complimentary statement

Confirmation and follow-up

Goodwill

Refusing a job offer

Hints for an ideal letter:

- Make an appreciation statement for the offer.
- Formally state your inability to accept the offer.
- Don't brag if you received a better offer elsewhere.
- Generally try to offer a neutral reason for the refusal.
- Appreciate the time and efforts of the people who met with you or provided information about the company.

Dear Mr. Winfield:

Thank you for your offer to become part of the quality assurance team at Henneger-Brockton Labs. The dedicated and professional team that I met during the interviewing procedure is a group I would have been proud to join, since my skills and background would mesh nicely with theirs. — *Appreciation*

I will be unable to accept your offer because in the interim, I was invited to take a supervisory position at Wimbledon Laboratories. This is a positive career move and one that will develop additional skills for me. It is with reluctance that I tell you I am going to accept that position rather than the one at H-B. — *Formal "unable to accept" statement / Neutral tone*

I am very grateful for the time you spent with me and your candor in answering the questions I had. Everyone was most gracious, and I certainly hope we will have an opportunity to meet again in the future. — *Appreciation*

Resignation

What's wrong with this letter:

- Does not leave door open for future business association
- Negative, harsh tone
- Does not express gratitude for the company

WRONG WAY

Dear Mr. Wintergarden:

I hereby tender my resignation from Barton's Bank, effective June 4.

You know that I have been frustrated recently with our inability to implement our continuous improvement initiatives effectively and believe that a change in scenery will be in my best interests. I have not made any secret of my desire to obtain a master's degree in adult education, and I will receive my degree next month, which opens the door for me to pursue the career I really want.

I applied for and was offered a position to teach at the community college in the fall, but have now been asked to fill in for the person who was to have taught the summer session at the college. Apparently, this rather flaky individual abruptly took an overseas trip, leaving a vacancy. I had not anticipated leaving this soon, so it may seem rather sudden to you, but resigning will reduce the stress that has begun to affect my physical and mental well-being.

I am saddened to leave the many colleagues who have been part of my banking career, but am confident that a better future lies ahead for me.

Doesn't leave door open

Negative, harsh tone

No gratitude for company

Resignation

Hints for an ideal letter:

- Remember that you don't want to burn bridges, so keep the door open for future business association.
- Mention any reason for leaving that is a legitimate one.
- If there is an issue such as a personality conflict, anger, or unpleasant political matters, do not air it in this letter.
- Maintain a positive tone in the letter.
- Express gratitude for something the company has done.

RIGHT WAY

Dear Mr. Wintergarden:

My seven-year association with Barton's Bank has been a time of growing and learning, and I greatly value the personal and professional relationships that I have developed here. You know that I have been working toward a career goal of obtaining a master's degree in adult education, and a wonderful opportunity has come my way. I will receive my degree next month and have been offered a position to teach at the community college in the fall. — *Positive tone*

Here's the strange part! The person who was to have taught the summer session at the college abruptly took an overseas trip, leaving a vacancy that I was asked to fill. I had not anticipated leaving this soon, so it may seem rather sudden to you, but it will give me a chance to become comfortable with the college surroundings before we go full swing into fall. My official departure date will be May 30. — *Reason for leaving*

My delight at this extraordinary and serendipitous turn of events is tinged with considerable sadness at leaving the many wonderful friends I have made at the Bank. I know that the things I learned here will make me a better person for all the people I teach in the future. — *Positive tone*

Thank you for your support, your willingness to challenge me, and your assistance with my growth and development. I will remember my time at Barton's with great fondness. — *Gratitude*

Thank-you for interview

Hints for an ideal letter:

- Mention specifically what you discussed.
- Suggest something you learned or took away from the interview.
- Remind the interviewer of your strengths.
- Be polite and sincere (makes a lasting impression).
- Say again that you want the job.

Dear Ms. Freeburg:

I appreciate the time you took to meet with me yesterday and enjoyed hearing about the plans you have to develop more of a market share for Freeburg Realty. I thought your new slogan of "You're home free with Freeburg" was catchy and will certainly get people's attention. One of the intriguing parts of the interview for me was the structured orientation program for the newly licensed Realtors. Since I would participate in that, I felt that it is thorough and yet not confining.

After meeting several members of the Freeburg team, I was struck by the high degree of commitment, maturity, and collaborative attitude of the other Realtors. They made me feel welcome already. I think my excellent communication skills, loyalty, team spirit, enthusiasm, and dedication will fit right in. I want to reiterate my desire to become a member of Freeburg Realty.

Thank you for your interest and for letting me know that it will be two weeks before your decision is made. I look forward to hearing from you then. In the interim, if you need any additional information, please call me at xxx-xxxx.

Specific information

Something learned

Complimentary tone
Mention of strengths
Restatement of desire

Polite close

ADJUSTMENT LETTERS

Credit card billing error
Hints for an ideal letter:

- Be specific about what error occurred.
- Provide facts about what steps you have taken to remedy the situation.
- Tell the customer that you are available if there are problems in the future.

Dear Ms. Parker:

Thank you for notifying us of the duplicate charge to your MasterCard that appeared on your October billing. We contacted Ettinger's Department Store, which conducted some research internally and came up with the answer. They discovered that the duplication occurred when a new employee mistakenly transmitted the same transaction twice, thinking that the electronic register had not accepted it. The register in fact had entered your sale twice.

The staff at Ettinger's apologized for the error and assured us that additional training has been provided to the salesclerk in question. The Ettinger customer service representative also told us that she is mailing you a 20 percent one-time discount coupon for your next visit to the store.

Please let us know if we can help you in the future.

Pleasant tone

Specific reason for error

Apology
Something special

Offer of availability

Damage notification

Hints for an ideal letter:

- Acknowledge the customer's feelings.
- Identify who is responsible for the damage.
- State what corrective action has been taken or will be taken.
- Discuss follow-up.
- Apologize where appropriate.

Dear Mr. and Mrs. Otterman:

We know how eagerly you have awaited the arrival of your custom-made rolltop desk. We were dismayed, and we know that you will be also, to find that it was damaged (deep gouges in the wood on the side) when it arrived in our warehouse last week. While we were planning happily to inform you that it was delivered ten days early, we now must regretfully tell you that there will be a delay while the desk is remade.

The warehouse supervisor has determined that the damage occurred in the boxing process when the automated equipment accidentally came in contact with the desk. We have placed a rush order on the replacement, so that may expedite the building process by about two weeks.

When you placed your order, you deleted the built-in lamp because of the additional cost, so we have added that to your replacement order at no charge to you. We think you'll like your new desk even better than the first one. Right now, we anticipate that the desk will arrive on or before March 23.

We'll call you just as soon as it arrives to schedule delivery. Again, we apologize for the delay and ask that you call us if you have any questions at all.

Acknowledgment of feelings

Who was responsible
Corrective action

Something special given
Deadline
Follow-up
Apology

I love being a writer. What I can't stand is the paperwork.

— Peter De Vries

Adjusting policy
What's wrong with this letter:

- Uses a negative tone
- Does not mention that you value the customer
- Criticizes customers

To all of our valued customers:

Lo-Cost Office Supplies regrets the need to implement a very difficult business decision and must change one of our long-standing policies. As of June 1, we will no longer offer cash refunds for supplies and equipment. Your only option will be to accept an in-store credit for any items you need to replace. A receipt will be required for these transactions.

We will continue to accept company purchase orders, and returns will be credited toward future purchases. We hope that you understand that these changes were necessary because some customers took advantage of our goodwill, and unfortunately our good customers must now suffer because of them.

We look forward to continuing to meet all of your organizational supply needs. Please visit us soon!

WRONG WAY

Negative tone

Criticizes customers

No mention of customer value

Adjusting policy

Hints for an ideal letter:

- Clearly state how new rules/policies may have changed from what the customer received previously.
- Maintain a pleasant yet businesslike tone.
- Offer appreciation for their understanding or cooperation.
- Mention that you value your customer.

RIGHT WAY

To all of our valued customers:

Lo-Cost Office Supplies appreciates your past business and values the long-standing relationship we have had. To continue to offer you the lowest possible prices on all of your business and supply needs, we have made some changes to familiar policies.

As of June 1, we will no longer offer cash refunds for supplies and equipment. However, because your satisfaction is our greatest concern, we will allow in-store credit for any items you need to replace. Please bring your receipt to guarantee full credit. We will continue to honor company purchase orders, and returns will be credited toward future purchases. We hope that you understand that these changes are designed to keep prices low for you.

We look forward to continuing our business relationship and meeting all of your organizational supply needs. Please visit us soon!

Pleasant tone

Statement of valuing the relationship

Policy change

How it will work

Request for understanding

Restates customer value

Replacing merchandise

Hints for an ideal letter:

- Empathize with a customer's frustration.
- Express regret that the customer was not satisfied.
- State what you will do for your customer.
- Try to interest your customer in other products.
- If possible, offer a benefit to compensate for any disappointment.

Dear Ms. Koerner:

Thank you for being a catalog customer of the Happy Chef Kitchen Collection. We know that you have enjoyed many of our fine gourmet cooking utensils and products in the past. *[Value of the customer]*

We appreciate your letting us know that the Chef's Delight Bread Machine did not meet your expectations and regret that you were not successful in producing high-quality bread. Although it was probably frustrating, it is good that you did try making bread several times to guarantee that it was indeed the fault of the machine rather than the yeast, temperature, or ingredient mix. *[Expression of regret / Empathy]*

We will immediately credit your charge card for $137.95, which includes the shipping and handling fees. *[What will be done]*

I have also enclosed a copy of our hot-off-the-press summer catalog, which features dozens of new items. Check them out ... we think you'll find something unique that you will love! We'll offer you a one-time 25 percent discount on your next purchase and hope to receive your order soon. Just use the handy order form enclosed, or call us at 1-800-xxx-xxxx. *[Offer a benefit / Action step]*

COMPLAINT LETTERS

Billing error
Hints for an ideal letter:

- Identify the specific error.
- Ask for an immediate correction.
- Maintain a neutral rather than a critical or hostile tone.
- Provide facts: dates, dollar amounts, account numbers, check/credit card numbers, documentation of previous calls or letters you have exchanged.
- If possible, state a benefit to the vendor/seller of eliminating future errors.

Dear Customer Service Representative:

We at Hartco Engineering have purchased your copy machines exclusively for eight years. The reasons for that are not only a superior product but also your timely and courteous customer service. We do seem to be having trouble right now resolving an error in a billing from you and request that it be corrected immediately.

When we purchased the new XP-3800 three months ago, we also purchased the two-year service contract that will begin after your one-year warranty expires. The fee for that did appear on our invoice. However, we have now received two additional invoices (#7042 and #7138) for the amount of our old service contract on our previous copier. That copier was returned to you as a trade-in on our new machine. Therefore, you have it — we don't.

We spoke with Marcia Patterson in your office on August 12 after receiving the first bill, and she said the amount would be removed from your computer. Around September 10, we received a second bill for the same amount plus a late fee. Surely you can understand our frustration!

Please ensure that both the service contract fee and the late fee are removed, and we'll both save the time spent in phone calls and letters! Thank you very much for your help.

Neutral tone

Request for correction

Specific error

Facts

Additional details

Benefit in the future

> A sentence aimed at nothing always hits its mark.
>
> — John O'Hayre

Misunderstanding instructions
Hints for an ideal letter:

- Identify the specific problem.
- Be pleasant rather than hostile or critical.
- Provide appropriate facts.
- Ask for an immediate correction and other action steps.

Dear Erik:

I am faxing this letter to clarify and document for you my instructions on the pamphlet you are printing for Social Services. When I said that I wanted the material printed in both Spanish and English, I didn't mean in the same pamphlet. It is a clever way to eliminate extra paper, but as my staff reviewed the galley proofs, they discovered a problem. When the paper is folded, the reader isn't sure where to read next because the pages become intermixed. We think this will be more confusing than helpful.

Let me clarify that our department needs two separate pamphlets, one printed only in English and one printed only in Spanish. The agency has limited resources for this project, and we expect that you will pay for any additional typesetting expenses to produce two separate pamphlets.

We will want to see the galley proofs again, of course, so please fax me a revised printing schedule and a projected date for both the proofs and the finished print job.

Thanks very much for your help, Erik!

Pleasant tone

Specific problem

Facts

Clarification

Immediate correction and action steps

Appreciation

Lack of courtesy from an employee
Hints for an ideal letter:

- Specify the exact behavior that you felt was inappropriate.
- Use firm, clear language, but do *not* attack the employee.
- State your expectations about service provided by that organization.
- If you are going to pursue your complaint further, inform the reader of your intended actions (if applicable).

Dear Dr. St. Clair:

I have been a patient of yours for about six years and have always enjoyed coming into your office, even though trips to the dentist are not known to be high on everyone's list of favorite activities. Your staff has always been extremely courteous and friendly, and everyone goes out of the way to make patients feel comfortable and relaxed.

One of your newer employees, Jan, does not seem to treat the patients as the others do. I noticed it on a visit a month ago, but thought that maybe she was just having a bad day. Since it happened again when I brought my daughter in yesterday, I feel obligated to let you know about this because it affects your image.

Jan will not acknowledge with a look or smile a patient who enters the office. She didn't acknowledge me or three others who came in while I was sitting in the lobby. She does not say anything to any of the patients, and I have not ever seen her smile. I feel that being pleasant to a customer involves smiling and talking to the person. Even if she is uncomfortable making small talk, she could learn a few simple phrases and just use them over and over.

If you are concerned about the image of your office as presented by your staff, you may want to discuss the outer-office greeting behaviors with them. I want to continue looking forward to coming in to see you.

- *Pleasant tone*
- *Specific example*
- *Clear description of poor behavior*
- *Expectation of performance*
- *Continuing relationship*

Unsatisfactory performance

Hints for an ideal letter:

- Be clear about what was unsatisfactory.
- Provide details without sounding attacking.
- State your requirements simply and specifically.
- State your next action step (if applicable).

Dear Mr. Owen:

As the manager of the neighborhood maintenance department for the city of Monterey, you need to be aware of situations where your employees do not perform up to expectations. I called your office two weeks ago to tell you about a huge pile of tinder-dry brush and weeds that lines the backs of the wooden fences of the homes on my street. According to the local television stations, there is an extreme fire danger right now, and they are cautioning everyone to be extremely careful. I am worried about the fire hazard since it would take only a small spark to send this entire neighborhood into flames.

The receptionist referred me to one of your staff, Mr. John Killibrew, who promised to visit the site that afternoon and call me back. When I checked with him three days later, he said he had been busy and would drive out here by the end of the week. He did not do this. By the next week, I was calling him every day, and he would not return my phone calls. We are now into the third week of extremely hazardous conditions, with no action.

I would like you to now become involved and assign this case to an employee who will help us remove the brush. I do not want to call the city manager's office, but I will have to do that if I cannot get action from your department. Thank you for your attention to this matter. I hope to hear from you by August 25 regarding your resolution of my complaint.

Introduction of problem (background)

Expression of concern

Specific details

State required action

Unsatisfactory product/service

Hints for an ideal letter:

- Specify your complaint about the product or service.
- Ask for specific changes.
- Emphasize a benefit of quick resolution.

Dear Mr. Cohen:

We have been very excited about offering our employees the use of Cohen's Fitness Center and Gym during their lunch hour and after-work hours. We set up this contract as part of our Employee Wellness and Stress-Free Work Environment Program and have publicized it extensively. The response has been phenomenal. However, our employees have informed us of a problem we had not anticipated. — *Introduction*

Originally, we set up our contract with you to provide a designated area where our employees would have sole use of the machines without any of your other customers using them at the same time. Apparently, this is not happening, and our employees are having to wait. This is causing a problem because of their limited lunch hour. We will need to see this resolved immediately. — *Complaint*

Here is what needs to happen:
1. The designated area must be kept free for city employees.
2. If more area is needed, we will renegotiate the terms of our contract to make that happen.
3. We will be monitoring fitness-center use very closely for the next 30 days to see trends.
4. We will be using a feedback form for our employees to tell us about their experience at the center.

— *Changes needed*

We want to see positive results happen over the next 30 days. At that time, we will determine if we wish to extend the program for two years. We are looking forward to a strong and positive association with Cohen's since good health and stress reduction are everyone's goals today. — *Quick resolution*

COLLECTION LETTERS

Gentle reminder
Hints for an ideal letter:

- Assume the customer has sent a payment that crossed in the mail.
- Use positive language.
- Remind the customer of the specifics: date, amount, etc.
- Close with a thank-you.

Dear Mr. Wilson:

As of September 30, we have not yet received your August 15 payment. You may have already mailed this, or perhaps it was just overlooked if you have been busy.

Please check your records, and disregard this notice if your payment indeed was sent. Thank you for your attention.

Specifics

Assume payment was made

Stronger reminder

Hints for an ideal letter:

- Use positive language.
- Remind the customer of the importance of good credit.
- Ask if there is a problem you are unaware of.
- Offer to help.
- Restate the need to send the payment immediately.

Dear Mr. Wilson:

You have been a valued customer of Millennium Computer Superstores for three years and have an excellent history of prompt payment of monthly billings. I'm sure you are familiar with the 30-day terms for your account, with a designated payment due on a specific date with interest charges accruing after the payment date passes. — *Positive tone*

Your good credit rating is one of your most important assets, and we have been happy to serve as a reference when you have applied for credit elsewhere. To maintain that positive record, sending your monthly payment on time is imperative. — *Reminder of credit importance*

Is there a problem that we don't know about? Sometimes, for specified periods of time, we can waive the total payment in favor of paying interest only. This usually lasts for about three months. — *Ask about potential problem*

By sending your monthly payment of $150 for August and $150 for September immediately, plus the accrued interest of $23.87, you will retain your good credit rating and bring your account up to date. If we need to consider the "interest-only" plan because of special circumstances, please call me within 48 hours. I will be happy to help you set it up. — *Send now / Offer of help*

Request for an explanation
Hints for an ideal letter:

- Avoid threats, but send the message that you wish to collect the overdue amount immediately.
- Specifically request an explanation for nonpayment.
- Use stern but professional language.

Dear Mr. Wilson:

    We have not heard from you regarding your past-due status on your account. There are two outstanding monthly payments due plus accrued interest, and the due date for the next payment is fast approaching. *— Reminder*

    We do want to help you bring this account into a "current" status, so that we can retain our positive relationship. It is very important to resolve this now. *— Resolve now (strong language)*

    We need to know the reason for the lack of payment. As stated in a previous letter, if you have a problem at the present time, we will work with you on a payment schedule to maintain your account. We just need to know what has occurred so that we can determine the best course of action for you. Please remit your unpaid balance, or call us by close of business on October 25 to clarify this matter. *— Ask for reason for nonpayment / Deadline*

    We look forward to your call.

HOW TO CREATE HIGH-IMPACT LETTERS, MEMOS, AND E-MAIL

Appeal for payment
Hints for an ideal letter:

- Use stern language.
- Mention that more serious action will be necessary if the situation is not resolved. Provide deadlines.
- Keep it short.

Dear Mr. Wilson:

Your overdue account has been forwarded to me by our manager of Receivables, along with a record of the attempts we have made to determine the reason for nonpayment. They have been very tolerant with this situation and have made every effort to assist you in bringing your account up to date. *— Reminder*

Right now, there are three past-due payments and accrued interest totaling $502.43. This is not acceptable. If the payment is not received by the date below, we will initiate steps to repossess the equipment. *— Stern language*

I request an immediate payment of the outstanding amount no later than November 15. Thank you for your cooperation. *— Request for payment / Deadline*

Last call for payment (with stated consequences)

Hints for an ideal letter:

- Briefly review the record of attempts to receive payment.
- Use severe but businesslike language.
- State specific consequences.
- Mention that you regret the turn of events, which leaves the door open for your customer to return with dignity.

Dear Mr. Wilson:

Millennium Computer Superstores has made four attempts to reconcile the outstanding payments on your account. We have offered to assist you if this is a difficult time, we have suggested a payment schedule of interest-only, and we have been more than patient in waiting for your response.

You received a request for payment by November 15, and it is now December 2. We have not yet heard from you, so we are initiating repossession procedures on your equipment as stated in your original credit agreement. On December 5, members of our staff will arrive at your office by 9:30 a.m. to obtain:

1. 1 LZ4000 Computer
2. 2 ink-jet color printers
3. 1 laser printer
4. 2 printer stands
5. 4 interface cables

We had hoped to avoid this embarrassing situation for you by resolving the outstanding debt. It is regretful that a long-term business association is at risk, but we were left with no other options than to take extreme action.

We appreciate your cooperation in having the designated equipment ready for our representatives.

Review record

Reminder

Consequences

Specifics

Leave door open

SYMPATHY LETTERS

Acknowledgment of sympathy letter received
Hints for an ideal letter:

- Acknowledge all sympathy expressions — assistance, flowers, cards, and contributions.
- Send handwritten notes when replying to personal expressions of sympathy.
- Send typewritten responses on business letterhead when replying to a typed message from someone outside your organization.
- Thank the person for the act of kindness — letter, flowers, or donations.
- Include your personal thoughts about the deceased.
- Graciously accept or decline any offer of help.

Dear Gina,

Thank you for sharing your kind thoughts about my mother. Your letter means a great deal to me at this time.

I feel as though I've lost not only my mother but also my best friend. Whenever I needed a sounding board, she was there to listen. Whenever I needed support, she was there to give it. A daughter could not have asked for a more loving and caring mother.

I so appreciate your covering my accounts during the next two weeks, particularly with the workload you're already handling. It's at times like this when I realize how fortunate I am to work with such a thoughtful associate. Know that I'm most grateful.

Personal thanks

Your thoughts

Acceptance of offer to help

Death

Hints for an ideal letter:

- Handwrite your message on personal stationery.
- Make it sincere and comforting.
- Offer your condolences (first part).
- Give a personal recollection of the person who has died (second part).
- End with an offer of help and any memorial being made.

Dear Marta,

    I am greatly saddened to hear of Roger's death and wish to extend my sympathy. His passing is such a loss. — *Condolences*

    I'll never forget first meeting Roger during my orientation. Even though it's been ten years, I still remember how warmly he greeted me, introduced me to the department staff, and gave me a personal tour of the office. He took the time to review the company's history and patiently explained all policies and procedures. He assured me his door would always be open and encouraged me to call on him whenever I needed assistance. — *Personal recollection*

    From that first day, Roger became my role model. I marveled at his ability to put customers at ease, to win their trust, and to establish solid partnerships. I benefited from his wisdom, his guidance, and his expertise. He gave so much of himself and asked for so little in return. — *Further recollection*

    As a way of remembering him, please accept this collection of photographs and articles highlighting his career. May you take some comfort in knowing how important Roger was to the people who had the opportunity to work with him. — *Additional condolences and memorial gift*

    My thoughts and prayers are with you.

Terminal illness

Hints for an ideal letter:

- Convey a thoughtful, caring tone.
- Avoid mentioning the illness and any chance for recovery.
- Comment on the daily pleasures the reader can still enjoy.

Dear Tillie,

   Herb just called and gave me an update on how you are doing. I'm glad to know you're receiving special care from the doctors and nurses. It sounds like you are in good hands.

   I understand that you are enjoying the ceramics classes and that you've created a variety of cups, bowls, and vases. And to think that several people have asked about purchasing them! If you need a sales representative, remember me!

   I'm looking forward to seeing you so we can catch up. I'll call you next week to check on the best time for a visit.

   Rest comfortably, and know that you're in my thoughts.

Caring tone

Special pleasure reader enjoys

Sincere wish

> Nothing you write, if you hope to be good, will ever come out as you first hoped.
>
> — Lillian Hellman

Illness/injury

Hints for an ideal letter:

- Convey how sorry you are to hear of the illness or injury.
- Have an upbeat tone; avoid sounding morose.
- Reassure that all work responsibilities will be covered (if the person will be returning to work).
- Extend get-well wishes.

Dear Chad:

   I just learned about your recent back surgery and am thankful to know that you are recovering well. *(Personal concern)*

   I can imagine your stay in the hospital is a far cry from your life on the road. But I bet you're not missing the airports, the rental cars, the hotels, and the room service menus! Let's face it — sleeping in the same room for a few weeks, eating balanced and nutritious meals, and striking up new friendships with the hospital staff must be a welcome change. Plus it's a chance for you to get some needed rest and spend some quality time with Christine and the kids. *(Upbeat tone)*

   I'm looking forward to seeing you in the next week. I'll plan to stop by one afternoon after the doctors have made their rounds. Have some stories ready! *(Note about work / Good wishes)*

Illness (cont.)

Dear Melissa:

    I am relieved to know that your automobile accident was not more serious. Thank goodness you were wearing a seatbelt and driving a car with an air bag! — *Expression of concern*

    Jason tells me that your hospital stay was brief and that you are resting comfortably at home. He also says that you are following doctors' orders — as well as his. I think his words were, "She's an excellent patient when she's asleep!" It sounds like you are in good hands. — *Positive tone*

    Several clients have called asking about you — Blake Crosby, Amanda Vordenbaumen, Truc Pham, and Elliot Wasserman. They miss your friendly voice, positive personality, and "can-do" attitude. So do I. — *Additional thoughts of concern*

    While you are recovering, Caroline Wong is handling your customer service and administrative responsibilities and keeping track of me. No easy task, as you well know! Yet everything seems to be under control — at least for the moment. — *Workload covered*

    Take the time you need to get better and rest well. — *Sincere wishes*

WRITING EFFECTIVE MEMOS

General format

Memos are different from letters in that they are primarily meant to be internal communications used to manage the information flow in organizations. Memos typically used to be paper-copy documents, although e-mail (electronic mail) has more recently become a critical element in the internal communication process.

Memos may have the businesslike tone of formal announcements or may have the warm, personal tone of casual conversation. Depending upon the culture and climate, either more formal or more informal can be appropriate. Many companies and government agencies have a preestablished format for their memos, but if not, use the following general guidelines:

MEMORANDUM

MEMO DATE: Correct date

TO: Name(s) of recipient

FROM: Name of sender

RE: Subject of the memo

COPIES TO: Distribution list — optional

```
Memo text here — use normal paragraph or bullet-point
```
- Many of the software programs used in today's offices have memo templates built into the programs that will work fine. The templates will have preset margins and headings, generally requiring only your text to be input.

- Use the following guidelines if you will be creating your memo format(s) yourself.

Margins
- Use one-inch side margins.
- Use a two-inch top margin.
- Start your headings three lines below the letterhead.
- Set a tab so that text will block on the left. There should be two spaces between the longest heading and the tab.

Headings
- When you identify yourself on the "From" line of the memo, you may add other information such as:

  Department:
  Floor No.:
  Phone No.:
  Fax No.:

- Always type headings in all capital letters (even in bold print if you have that option). Follow each item with a colon.

- Personal titles (Mr., Mrs., Ms.) are generally not used in memos. In very casual memos, sometimes only a first name appears.

Body of the memo
- Start typing three lines below the last heading line.
- Do not place a salutation in the body of the memo.

- Type memos single-spaced, and block all lines to the left margin, or indent one-half inch on the first line of each paragraph.
- Leave one blank line between paragraphs.

Signatures
- Memos do not normally require a signature line. Many writers think this is impersonal and like to use a signature line anyway. If you need a signature, type the writer's name or initials on the second line below the end of the message. If you plan to fill in a handwritten name or initials as well, type the signature line four lines below the end of the message.
- Omit the signature line if you handwrite initials next to the typed name in the heading.

Optional notations
If you use additional notations, place them in the following order, after the body copy, according to whatever combination you choose:
1. Reference initials
2. File notation (it's very common to see the computer file name)
3. Enclosure notation
4. Copy notation (if different from a distribution list shown at the top of the memo)

Confidential notation
- If a confidential notation is needed, type it in all-capital letters and bold print if possible, three lines below the heading.
- Begin the body of the memo three lines below this notation.

Continuation pages
Many writers pride themselves on the ability to write a one-page memo, but if you need two or more pages, use the same style as outlined in the formats for letters.

Quick tips for readable memos
1. Use short paragraphs — they are easy to read and comprehend for fast action.
2. Use subheadings to identify blocks of information — readers love it, since they can skim the material.
3. Use white space — the appearance of your memo is important.
4. Be a fanatic about spelling — even one little misspelled word hurts your credibility.
5. Answer all reader questions — use "who, what, where, when, why, and how" to cover the bases.
6. Avoid acronyms, jargon, and buzz talk — memo writers love to fill space with these, and readers hate them if they don't know the meaning.
7. Create a positive tone wherever possible — a memo is not the place to take out your frustration about red tape.
8. Be concise — short, simple, and to-the-point are musts for a great memo.
9. Use down-to-earth language — technical or legalistic verbiage turns off the reader.
10. Double-check grammar, punctuation, sentence length, agreement of subjects and verbs, and all other grammatical fine points.

SAMPLE MEMOS

I keep six honest serving men (They taught me all I knew): Their names are What and Why and When and How and Where and Who.

— Rudyard Kipling

Announcement of new staff member
Hints for an ideal memo:

- Briefly present appropriate facts/information.
- State action steps, if any.

MEMORANDUM

DATE: March 10, 19xx

TO: All members of the Purchasing Department

FROM: Allan Winter, manager

RE: New staff member – Our analyst position has finally been filled!

Anne Greenwood will join our department on Monday, March 14, as the new purchasing analyst II. Anne brings to us a diverse background with experience in accounting as well as purchasing. She was a former vice president of the IAPA (International Association of Purchasing Agents) and has slightly more than 11 years of experience in the field.

Anne has strong skills for our team, is a collaborative problem-solver, an energetic and enthusiastic individual, and a real detail person. She is looking forward to meeting all of you on Monday. Please give her a warm welcome and help her to find her way around.

Review facts

Complimentary tone

Action steps

MEMORANDUM

Date: April 1, 19XX

To: Members of the Finance Department
From: Vice president of finance
Re: New assistant director of finance

I am pleased to announce the April 1 promotion of Cathy Fisher to assistant director of finance. She will report directly to Fred Johnson, director of finance.

Cathy will be responsible for supervising all aspects of the company's accounting, purchasing, and budgeting procedures. She will assist the director in preparing sales projections and monitoring expenditures of all of the company's divisions.

Cathy began her career with our organization in 1990 as a financial analyst. After two years in that position, she was promoted to manager of the Accounting Department. During the time she headed our Accounting Department, she coordinated two audits by Cooper, Gray & Co. Both audits were exception-free, indicating her outstanding performance.

Cathy also has shown a strong commitment to pursuing her educational goals. She received her undergraduate degree in finance from Oregon State University. Just this past December, she was awarded a M.B.A. in finance, also from the University of Oregon.

Our department is fortunate to have Cathy as part of our upper-management team. I know she will excel in her new role and be instrumental in our achieving next year's objectives.

Please join me in congratulating Cathy on her promotion.

Announcement of job promotion

Hints for an ideal memo:

- Announce the promotion, including name, position title, effective date, and line of reporting.
- List the employee's responsibilities.
- Mention previous accomplishments.
- Ask employees to congratulate the employee.

Announcement of promotion

Responsibilities of new position

Previous accomplishments

Educational achievements

Positive expectation

Congratulations

HOW TO CREATE HIGH-IMPACT LETTERS, MEMOS, AND E-MAIL

MEMORANDUM

DATE: August 22, 19xx

TO: The computer operations staff

FROM: Barbara

RE: Upcoming training

I know that many of you have been looking forward to the upcoming conference in Chicago where the new hardware will be unveiled. Others have some of their professional development courses scheduled for the fall term at LJC. We have had an unexpected cutback in the budget money for all of our training and development that will affect you. Unfortunately, both conferences and seminars will be eliminated until at least October 1.

The cutback resulted from the poor numbers at the end of the second quarter that have extended well into our third quarter. The good news is that we will review this situation toward the end of September, and we may be able to reinstate some of the budget for the fourth quarter.

The tuition reimbursement fund was not affected, so if any of you will be taking evening courses on your own time, they will be covered according to the usual policy guidelines.

Let's all work together to have a great third quarter and look forward to doing our professional development during the fourth quarter.

Disappointing news for staff
Hints for an ideal memo:

- Start with a neutral tone; avoid a stuffy, pompous style.
- Offer rationale for the bad news before you give it.
- Find a positive side of the situation if possible.

Neutral tone

Rationale

Disappointing news

Additional rationale

Positive side

Goodwill

MEMORANDUM

DATE: February 8, 19xx

TO: The Employee Communications Committee

FROM: Dave

RE: Team meeting

OK, everybody ... the meeting leader rotation puts me up to bat this week for our meeting. Some new projects have been passed on from the director, so our agenda will be full. I've attached a copy of the proposed agenda, but as usual, we'll fine-tune it at the beginning of the meeting.

I'm suggesting a different time than normal because our meeting is the same day as the Employee Appreciation Lunch. The lunch will probably run a little longer than usual because of the awards portion at the end.

Time: 2:00 (don't show up at 1:00 like usual)
Date: February 11
Location: Lobby conference room

At this meeting, we must finalize our form for the Employee Satisfaction Survey, so please read the draft from the last meeting, delete the questions you don't like, and come armed with any other suggestions. We won't quit until we have the final survey form.

See you all on Thursday!

Notification of a team meeting
Hints for an ideal memo:
- Provide specific details.
- Mention preparation requirements.
- State outcomes for the meeting.

Introduction with casual tone

Details

Preparation requirements
Outcomes

Announcement of workshop

Hints for an ideal memo:

- Provide purpose and benefits of attending.
- Provide specific details.
- Request attendees to confirm their attendance.

MEMORANDUM

Date: September 1, 19XX

To: All employees

From: Director of Human Resources

Re: "Just How Safe Are You?" workshop

Do you ever think about your personal safety? *— Purpose*

For example, just how safe are you at work? At home? In your car? When you're traveling?

Now is the time to address these issues and learn steps you can take to keep you and your family safe! *— Benefits*

How?   By attending the "Just How Safe Are You?" workshop featuring Janis Howard, president of JH Security and former police chief of Saratoga.

What?   A "brown bag" lunch

When?   Tuesday, September 13, noon – 1:15 p.m. *— Meeting specifics*

Where?   Conference Room A

Come with a bag lunch. Beverages will be provided.

Seating is limited, so give Roy Holley a call at Ext. 6607 by September 9 to reserve a seat. You'll be glad you did! *— Request for confirming attendance*

MEMORANDUM

Date: June 1, 19XX

To: All employees

From: Executive director

Re: "Casual day" dress policy

Beginning June 6, Fridays will be "casual days." This is in response to recent requests from several employees. The management team believes the new dress code will boost morale and increase productivity throughout the week.

Projecting a professional image to our customers still rates as a priority. Since "casual" attire is subject to individual interpretation, the following guidelines need to be accepted by everyone for "casual day" to succeed.

- No shorts or cut-offs
- No jeans
- No sweatshirts, sweatpants, or sweatsuits
- No tee shirts with emblems or advertisements
- No tank tops
- No leggings

If you choose to wear any of the above items to the office, you will be asked to return home to change. The bottom line in selecting your casual dress is this — use professional judgment. If you are unsure whether certain attire is appropriate, check with your supervisor in advance.

I am convinced this policy change will be a popular one. Let's commit to following the guidelines so all of us can enjoy more casual Fridays.

Announcement of new policy

Hints for an ideal memo:

- State the new policy and the effective date.
- Use a positive tone, particularly if the policy conveys bad news.
- Offer a contact person who can give additional information or answer questions.
- Close by conveying appreciation for following the policy.

Statement of new policy and effective date

Specific details of policy

Contact person

Appreciation

MEMORANDUM

DATE: June 18, 19xx
TO: All company employees
FROM: Earl Bellman, executive vice president
RE: Policy on employee holidays

This memo will provide a few additional points about the information you received last week on our change in employee holidays. A number of staff members called with questions about the new "floating" holiday, and the details below should answer all of your issues.

What change occurred?
Instead of celebrating Columbus Day as a company, we have changed the nature of that holiday to one that an employee may take at any time in the year. It is called a "floating holiday." You may take it with any other vacation day or holiday, or on its own. The company will be open on Columbus Day.

May I work on that extra day and be paid overtime?
No. The intent of this holiday is to give you greater freedom with your time off. Your health and well-being are important to us, and to be healthy, you need downtime.

Am I eligible if I am a new employee?
Yes. You are eligible for this floating holiday after 90 days of continuous employment. That makes it available to everyone, with just a slightly longer wait for a few of you.

May I accumulate this holiday from year to year?
No. You must take your floating holiday within each calendar year.

These were the major questions we were asked after the memo was distributed. If you still have additional concerns, please call Sherry Goldman in human resources at Ext. 2341.

Clarifying a policy change
Hints for an ideal memo:

- Use clear, simple language.
- Be specific.
- Offer a resource if staff members have questions.

Specific clarification of change

Clear, simple language

Resource

MEMORANDUM

DATE: September 2, 19xx

TO: Ellen Schur, supervisor

FROM: Priscilla Ball, supervisor

RE: Cross-training on the receptionist duties

Ellen, this request will help both our departments with the telephone coverage at the front desk. My employee, Kelli, has told me that she has had trouble getting a relief person for her breaks and lunches. Her backup, Suzanne, is not always available when she is needed, so Kelli is somewhat in a bind.

Would you be willing to let me train one of your employees to cover the switchboard? I have seen that both Lori and Gillian are excellent with customers and have very pleasant voices, so either one would be fine. My rationale is that since many of the calls are for your staff members, Lori or Gillian may be able to answer some of the incoming questions rather than just forwarding callers to a voice mailbox. They are both familiar with many of the departmental procedures and would sound very knowledgeable to our customers.

Can we meet to discuss the cross-training? I suggest Tuesday, September 6 at 10:00 if your calendar is open.

Thanks for your help, Ellen. I know if we put our heads together, we'll find a great solution.

Requesting something from another department

Hints for an ideal memo:

- Be clear.
- Explain your rationale/need.
- Appreciate/thank your reader.

Introduction/background

Clear request

Rationale

Appreciation/thank-you

MEMORANDUM

DATE: September 5, 19xx

TO: Priscilla Ball, supervisor

FROM: Ellen Schur, supervisor

RE: Receptionist cross-training

I received your request, Priscilla, for employees to train for the receptionist desk. I agree that it makes sense to have someone familiar with the department fielding those questions when the reps are busy or away from the work area.

Gillian is the one who would be ready with the least need for training, but were you aware that she works only 28 hours per week? We will probably have to train Lori, too, just to make sure that someone is available when needed.

My calendar is open on the 6th, so let's take that 10:00 meeting time and set up a schedule along with some definitions of roles and responsibilities. The last thing I want is tension over who is supposed to do what and when ...

I believe that if we do a good planning job, the rotation should be fairly smooth, the stress on Kelli will be lessened, and Lori and Gillian will have a good development opportunity. See you tomorrow.

Response

Hints for an ideal memo:

- Acknowledge the writer's request.
- Agree to or refuse the request.
- Give reasons/rationale if appropriate.
- Express confidence in the outcome.

Acknowledgment

Agreement with request

Rationale/explanation

Further action

Confidence

HOW TO CREATE HIGH-IMPACT LETTERS, MEMOS, AND E-MAIL

MEMORANDUM

DATE: May 26, 19xx

TO: All employees

FROM: Walter Aarons, facilities manager

RE: Parking lot resurfacing

This is a reminder that our parking lot is being resurfaced starting June 1. Remember that NO employee cars will be allowed in the lot from June 1–5.

Your options for that time are as follows:

1. Public transportation — the bus stops on the corner of Second and Broadway.
2. Carpooling and parking on the street.
3. Getting dropped off by a friend/family member.
4. Bikes or motorcycles — just remember that there is no secure spot; you'll be parking on the street.

You'll like the new surface treatment, and it will be worth the wait. We appreciate your patience while we do our upgrading effort.

If you have questions about other parking or transportation options, please call me at Ext. 31. Thank you.

Reminder

Hints for an ideal memo:

- Give specific details: dates, times, etc.
- Appreciate the reader's cooperation.
- Offer a resource for questions.

Details

Options

Appreciation

Resource

WRITING EFFECTIVE E-MAIL

Electronic mail (e-mail) has become a vital communication vehicle for living and operating in a "global village." Employees are communicating with computer messages as frequently as with hard-copy memos or letters. E-mail is a wonderful way to confirm travel arrangements to Singapore; register for a conference in the United Kingdom (for the price of a local phone call); or send simultaneous messages to all your team members, your manager, and several customers. Your organization may have its own internal e-mail system, primarily for intra-company use, that is not accessible from the outside. You may also be able to send e-mail via the Internet both at home and at work. No matter what system you use, e-mail has advantages and disadvantages — typical of burgeoning technologies. Let's explore them.

Advantages of e-mail
- It speeds up response time.
- It encourages a more conversational tone than the sometimes stuffy or artificial style adopted by memo and report writers, since it's an informal mode of communication.
- It allows users to communicate worldwide inexpensively.
- It increases the willingness of busy people to send a message where they might not do so by telephone or traditional letters.
- It enhances users' ability to communicate with large audiences simultaneously (including quick and easy copies and "blind" copies).
- It is capable of forwarding messages and attaching other documents.
- It provides users with written confirmation of verbal commitments.

Disadvantages of e-mail
- Writers often neglect spelling, grammar, and punctuation rules.
- The subject of the message is not clearly defined. Readers who "scan" mail before looking at each message thoroughly may not know from the subject line what the content is.
- Some people "copy the world" in their message headers and fill others' mailboxes with unwanted information.
- Some writers may have a false sense of security. E-mail is NOT a "private" medium. Inside an organization, computer specialists and company management can access any message within the system. On the Internet, any provider through which your message passes can access it. In government agencies, e-mail is considered public information and can be requested for review by any citizen.
- Some writers don't use the traditional upper- and lowercase type style. Instead, they use all capital letters or all lowercase letters — a practice many readers consider rude and unprofessional.
- Writers may clog organizational systems with inappropriate personal messages, such as jokes, recipes, weather reports, gossip, birthday or anniversary wishes, or "love notes."
- Overuse of e-mail may lead to a decline in the ability to produce professional documents, such as letters and memos that are still required in more traditional offices.
- If writers ignore the proper use of spelling, punctuation, and grammar in e-mail messages, they may carry over these bad habits to formal documents.

HOW TO CREATE HIGH-IMPACT LETTERS, MEMOS, AND E-MAIL

SUGGESTIONS FOR USING E-MAIL EFFECTIVELY

1. **Address the message correctly using the proper style.**

- Follow this format for an e-mail address to a specific person using the Internet:

    johndoe@anysite.com

- Use the typical heading for internal messages:

    From: Pete Burrell
    Sent: Friday, November 13, 1998
             2:34 p.m.
    To: Kristine Wharton
    Subject: Preparation needed for the
             team meeting on
             Wednesday, November 18

Most systems will allow you to create an "address book" of frequently used addresses which are then accessible with a single keystroke to fill in the heading block.

2. **Write a subject heading that is brief but clear.**

A common complaint from readers is finding cryptic subject lines in their e-mail messages. They then must read an entire message to determine the nature of the information. That may take more time than readers want to invest. By making your subject heading specific, readers can scan their messages — reading urgent action items immediately and saving less important messages for later.

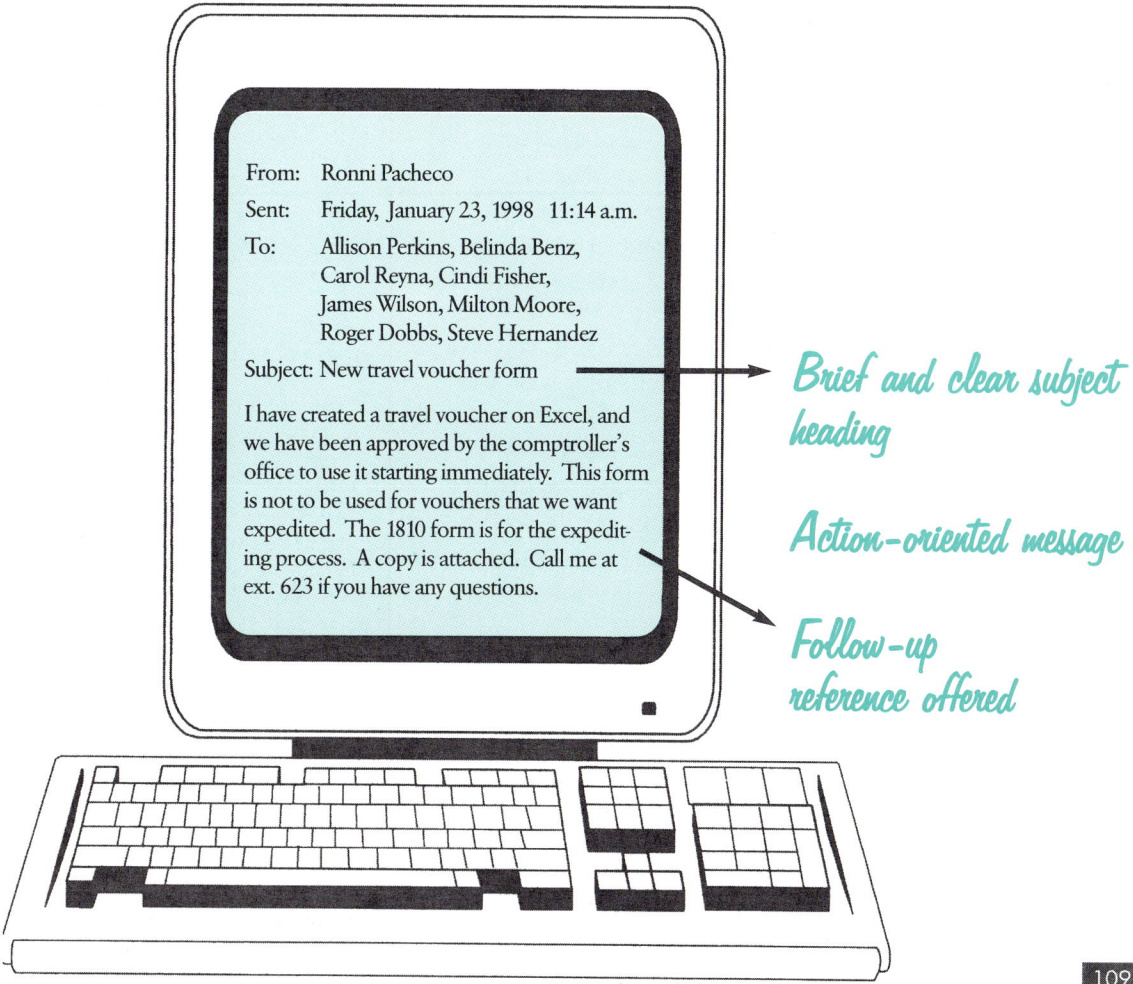

Brief and clear subject heading

Action-oriented message

Follow-up reference offered

HOW TO CREATE HIGH-IMPACT LETTERS, MEMOS, AND E-MAIL

From: Kelly Eichhorn
Sent: Tuesday, October 10, 1997 4:22 p.m.
To: John Emery, Susan Lamberto, Denise White, Bart LeBrun, Kyle Callaway, Brian Sears, Mark Shilgalis, Kiersten Hadley
Subject: Meeting schedule for 2Q98 pilots

Attached is the 2Q98 pilot strategy meeting schedule. Please note that the meeting will start at 11 a.m. instead of 8 a.m. Bring your "hot idea" folder and any input you have received from other departments or the field. We will work through lunch and have ordered pizzas for noon.

Clear subject line

Specific details

From: Carol Byrd
Sent: Monday, February 16, 1998 10:13 a.m.
To: Terry Hayek, Todd Gearhart, Janelle Green, Martha Jez, Patty Rodriguez, Gayla Coffey, Kevin Hixson, Renee LeJacque, Anne Banner, Bill Creighton
Subject: Temporary administrative assistant for the Compliance Division

The Compliance Division has hired Jean Helm as a temporary assistant while Becky is on leave. Jean will be with us for four weeks and will be working in Becky's office. Please welcome her, introduce yourself, answer questions she may have, and let her know how she can help you. Thanks for your cooperation.

Clear subject heading

Specific request

Pleasant, courteous tone

3. Organize your thoughts logically just as you would if you were writing a letter or memo.

Professional tone

Logical flow of information

From: Carrie Bellman
Sent: Friday, November 7, 1997 8:55 a.m.
To: All Exchange users, all PC Mail users
Subject: Company electronic mail policy

The following is PBE's policy on electronic mail (e-mail). This policy is taken directly from page eight of the Employee Manual, and we ask you to please respect it when you are using the company-wide e-mail system.

E-mail is designed to facilitate communication within the company. Limit your use of it to company business. It is not to be used for personal messages, jokes, or other unprofessional communication. Take care to use the same standards in drafting e-mail messages as you would in drafting memoranda for circulation within the company. The company reserves the right to review all electronic records, including e-mail, in the company computer network.

If you need to review this policy further and do not have your Employee Manual available, you may pick up a copy in the Human Resources Department.

Thank you.

Fourth message

From: Katherine Cook (kcook@appliedmanagement.com)
Sent: Wednesday, May 13, 1998 2:10 p.m.
To: Dan Stodghill
Subject: Training agenda for June 2 – 3

Dan, here is the program agenda you requested. The training is scheduled to run from 8 a.m. to 5 p.m. both days. You can see that we are focusing primarily on practice sessions.

Day One		Day Two	
8:00 – 8:30	Welcome, introduction, logistics	8:00 – 9:00	Develop product presentation plans
8:30 – 9:00	Overview of the training	9:00 –11:45	Program practice (Mimi)
9:00 – 11:45	Program practice (Jason)	11:45 – 1:00	Lunch
11:45 – 1:00	Lunch	1:00 – 1:30	Debrief morning
1:00 – 1:30	Debrief morning	1:30 – 4:00	Program practice (David)
1:30 – 4:00	Program practice (Dan)	4:00 – 5:00	Debrief afternoon/determine action items
4:00 – 5:00	Debrief afternoon		

Instructors — We have assigned you specific sections of the workbook to teach during your assigned program practice, but you should learn the entire program. The assignments are as follows:

Jason: Pages 1 – 9   Dan: Pages 10 – 17   Mimi: Pages 18 – 24   David: Pages 25 – 28

I will be on vacation until May 25, but Ella Bryan can answer any of your questions while I'm gone. Call her at ext. 2374, or e-mail her at ellbry@applied management.com.

———Response from Dan Stodghill———

Third message

From: Dan Stodghill
Sent: Wednesday, May 13, 1998 11:13 p.m.
To: Katherine Cook (kcook@appliedmanagement.com)
Subject: Presenting at the June training session

Katherine, I do plan to present. What is my assignment?

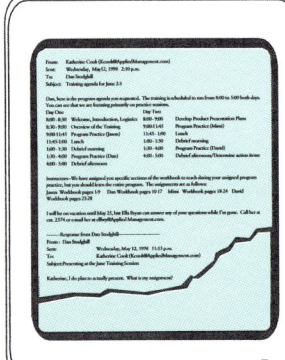

If you are responding to a previous message, use the REPLY key after briefly reviewing your original message. You'll keep the communication focused and avoid rambling. Note how the following messages reply to the previous communication.

E-mail (cont.)

———Response from Katherine Cook———
From: Katherine Cook (kcook@appliedmanagement.com)
Sent: Wednesday, May 13, 1998 8:56 a.m.
To: Dan Stodghill
Subject: Training for June 2–3

Second message

Dan, I will be happy to e-mail you a schedule before I leave today. Are you planning to present or will you be observing only? If you want to train, we will assign you a section of the program to learn. If not, we'll assign just Mimi, Jason, and David. Please respond before noon. Thanks!

———Original Message———
From: Dan Stodghill
Sent: Wednesday, May 13, 1998 6:49 a.m.
To: Katherine Cook
Subject: Upcoming training

First message

What is the agenda for the two-day training coming up in June? Will you let me know the specific times, please? I am impressed with the work you have done so far on the course materials, and I think this will be an easy course to teach. Thanks for your help on the agenda. Dan.

4. **Think carefully about who needs to be copied.**

   Some writers add unnecessary names to the "copies to" block without analyzing the reason for sending those copies. That floods others' e-mail boxes with mail, causing them to waste time reviewing and deleting the messages.

5. **Be cautious about your e-mail use.**

   Computer viruses have become as serious as plagues were to previous generations. Computer users have experienced corrupted systems and files that have cost millions (and potentially billions) of dollars to fix. Don't be a carrier!

The following e-mail sample contains information circulated throughout a government agency by the in-house Information Systems specialist detailing a real virus that is currently infecting e-mail readers.

From: Chuck Courtney
Sent: Thursday, February 5, 1998   10:45 a.m.
To: All agency employees
Subject: Macro virus

For those of you who are using Microsoft Word, I want to warn you that a virus is spreading through the program. Please be aware of e-mails containing any of the messages below. It is quite likely that you may get this from people outside the agency who use your e-mail address. Although nothing has been said about the proliferation of this virus through the Internet, I believe it is possible to contract it in this manner. Also, if you are getting Word documents from people outside the agency on disks, please let me know so we can thoroughly check these out. Here's what to look for:

Macro name: ShareFun.A

This macro virus spreads by infecting Word documents in Microsoft Word Versions 6.0 and 7.0 on Windows and Macintosh platforms. The virus consists of these macro names in infected documents:
AutoExec, AutoOpen, FileClose, FileExit, FileOpen, FileSave, FileTemplates, ShareTheFun, and ToolsMacro

The virus becomes active by using the Auto and System Macros shown above. After the virus has infected your system, there is a 25 percent chance that the following activities will occur. First the macro virus will save a copy of itself. Then it will check to see if you are running Microsoft Mail. If so, the virus will find three random people in your mail list and send a copy of the infected document with the following subject line: "You have GOT to read this!"

If Word is launched to read the attached file, the receiver will become infected and the above process will begin again. Therefore, if you receive a message with the subject or banner: "You have GOT to read this!," do not execute its attachment. Delete the entire message immediately.

Do not attempt to look at the macros. Both the ToolsMacro and FileTemplates will activate the virus. The macro FileSave is copied to the Global Template file NORMAL.DOT. If they are stored in NORMAL.DOT, they are available in all open documents. At this point, the macro viruses try to spread themselves to other documents. Macro viruses spread easily through e-mail packages. The ability of these packages to send and quickly launch documents can infect hundreds of users at a time. Documents are much more mobile than executable files, passing from machine to machine as different people write, edit, or access them. Macro viruses can, therefore, spread very quickly through business offices and corporations.

HOW TO CREATE HIGH-IMPACT LETTERS, MEMOS, AND E-MAIL

6. **Remember what your English teacher taught you.**

Grammar, spelling, and punctuation are just as important in e-mail as in a letter or memo that will be widely circulated among discriminating business readers. Your reputation is at stake since people are judging your competence, credibility, and professionalism as they read your message. Authors of e-mail messages often type so rapidly, as their thoughts skip ahead, that they make careless keyboarding typos and misspellings.

WRONG WAY

From: Michael Moody
Sent: Monday, March 23, 1998 11:22 a.m.
To: Ivan Wilson
Subject: E-mail notes

As we we discused yesterday, I am follolowing up with you concerning the instructions you neeeded to send e-mails via the internet.. I WAS TRYING TO BE BRIEF AND WASNT SUCCESSFUL—HAHA.....I WILL GIVE YOUUU TWO DIFFERENT SENARIOS FOR PEOPLE YOU WOULD- N'T COMMUNICTE WIRHT VERY FREQUENTLY AND ANOTHER FOR FOR WHEN YOU WANT TO HAVE SOMEONE IN YOUUR ADDRES BOOOK.
1/) SINGLE USE OF A E-MAIL ADDRESS
You would tyype (SMTP: username@domain.xxx) Type this wothout spaces and use a colon (not a semicolon) to separate the SMTp and the user- name.Also note that you enclose the typed text address within open anand closed brackets.
2) Regular communiation with someone
* Select "Book" icon in the MicroSoft Exchange wwindow.
* Select "Ppersonal Addres Book" (youu are adding an entry)
* Select "Neww Entry"
* Selct "internet Mail address"—click OK
* Enter the dispalu name and Iinternet Mail address (The display name is how the name appears in the "TO" field whhen you are creating a message.
Note: You don't have to type the open or closed brackets or the SMTP. IF YOU HAVE QUESTIONS<PLEASE LET ME KMOW>.

RIGHT WAY

From: Michael Moody
Sent: Monday, March 23, 1998 11:22 a.m.
To: Ivan Wilson
Subject: How to create e-mail addresses

As we discussed yesterday, I am following up with you concerning the instructions you need to send e-mails via the Internet. I will explain two different situations: There is one way to address mail to someone you rarely communicate with and another way to address mail by creating an entry in an address book on your computer. Use this for people you plan to send mail to frequently.
1.) Single use of an e-mail address
   Type (SMTP: username@domain.xxx). Type this without spaces and use a colon (not a semicolon) to separate the SMTP and the username. Also note that you enclose the typed text address within brackets.
2.) Frequent communication with someone
   * Select the "Book" icon in the Microsoft Exchange window.
   * Select "Personal Address Book" (you are adding an entry).
   * Select "New Entry."
   * Select "Internet mail address" – click OK.
   * Enter the display name and Internet mail address. (The display name is how the name appears in the "TO" field when you are creating a message.)
Note: You don't have to type the brackets or the SMTP for addresses listed in your personal address book. If there are any other questions I can answer for you, please call me, and I will do my best to help.

115

7. Think about the secondary reader.

Because of the ease of forwarding messages, receivers of e-mail often pass their mail on to others. The new reader is called a secondary reader. Another kind of secondary reader is someone with access to files where hard copies of e-mails are kept as documentation of a project, program, task, meeting, etc. Businesspeople are accustomed to keeping memos in their files, and with today's electronic communication, they still want something printed for future reference. No matter who the secondary reader is, be careful about automatically sending a writer's e-mail to another reader. Why? Some writers have suffered negative consequences when secondary readers have read messages that the authors never expected would be seen by anyone else.

8. Clearly state action items or deadlines.

A common complaint from writers is a lack of response from readers. E-mail readers do not know how to prioritize requests for actions that say "at your convenience," "ASAP," "in the near future," or "soon." They usually will respond to specific times and dates, as well as stated action items.

Poor wording:
  Please get the minutes to me ASAP.

More effective wording:
  Please send me a copy of the minutes from the May 18 meeting no later than June 10.

Anecdotal evidence suggests that readers read, respect, and respond as asked when requests state the specific action needed, a deadline for that action, and a reason for the request.

9. Don't offend readers.

Readers are frustrated by writers who refuse to use the shift key. Of course it's easier and faster not to hit that key. However, writers who won't capitalize even proper nouns or WHO SHOUT BECAUSE THE CAPS LOCK KEY IS ON annoy their readers. The easiest and fastest type style to read is still a combination of upper and lower case.

10. Follow your organizations' policy.

Most organizations have clear, well-defined policies about how e-mail is to be used. According to one of the largest newspapers in the United States, many employers review employee e-mail, and they have specific e-mail policies regarding this. Your organization is concerned about its image and how you present yourself in writing. Use the technology in a way that will uphold that image.

HOW TO CREATE HIGH-IMPACT LETTERS, MEMOS, AND E-MAIL

WRONG WAY

FROM: TERRY HERR
SENT: MONDAY, APRIL 6, 1998 8:23 A.M.
TO: JIM HAYDON
SUBJECT: QUESTIONS YOU'LL WANT TO ASK YOUR NEW EMPLOYER

JIM, HERE ARE THE MOST IMPORTANT QUESTIONS FOR YOU TO ASK AS YOU NEGOTIATE WITH YOUR NEW COMPANY:

1. IF I HAVE DIAL-UP ACCESS ON THE CORPORATE NETWORK, WILL THIS PROVIDE ACCESS TO MY E-MAIL?
2. WILL THE CORPORATE SYSTEM ALLOW ME TO SEND ATTACHMENTS WITH MY E-MAIL?
3. WHEN I'M WORKING IN ATLANTA, WILL I HAVE ACCESS TO EITHER A NETWORKED OR PERSONAL PRINTER TO PRINT MEMOS OR OTHER DOCUMENTS?
4. WILL I HAVE A FAX/MODEM ON THE LAPTOP?

PLEASE LET ME KNOW IF I CAN SUGGEST ANYTHING ELSE.

RIGHT WAY

From: Terry Herr
Sent: Monday, April 6, 1998 8:23 a.m.
To: Jim Haydon
Subject: Questions you'll want to ask your new employer

Jim, here are the most important questions for you to ask as you negotiate with your new company:

1. If I have dial-up access on the corporate network, will this provide access to my e-mail?
2. Will the corporate system allow me to send attachments with my e-mail?
3. When I'm working in Atlanta, will I have access to either a networked or personal printer to print memos or other documents?
4. Will I have a fax/modem on the laptop?

Please let me know if I can suggest anything else.

E-MAIL ETIQUETTE

The following hints on e-mail use are meant to help you use the computer efficiently and professionally, and to take advantage of its instant connection to readers. E-mail is a highly informal medium, but it still requires a "code of conduct." Strengthen your communication skills in the fine art of "Net-iquette."

Tips:

- Respond promptly. Readers appreciate same-day response, but when that isn't possible, responding within 48 hours is considered courteous.

- Use the "Reply" feature rather than generating a new message. This allows both your e-mail address and the recipient's to appear on the response.

- Be sensitive to confidential, highly personal, or incriminating information in a computer. Laws governing Internet use are continually evolving, and few privacy laws for e-mail have been developed and tested in court.

- If you will be sending files in an attachment, ask the reader if the format you are using is acceptable, since there may be difficulty downloading such files. If you receive unsolicited files, be wary of opening them. You may be exposing your system to a computer virus. Unsolicited files also clog disk space — keep this in mind if space is in short supply.

- Junk mail is junk mail. Electronic junk mail is generated when you give an e-mail address to a commercial site that places you on a mailing list for unsolicited mail. Avoid entering Web sites that require you to complete a request for information, such as your e-mail address.

- Don't use all capital letters. Most Net users consider this rude and unprofessional.

REFERENCE

Forms of address

When addressing letters to individuals, couples, professionals, and college and university officials, follow these suggested forms of address and salutation.

When writing to a ...	Inside address	Salutation
Woman	Ms./Miss/Mrs. Paula Stevenson	Dear Ms. Stevenson:
Man	Mr. Ted Bell	Dear Mr. Bell:
Two women	Ms. Carol Fisher Ms. Cathy Stella	Dear Mses. Fisher and Stella:
Two men	Mr. James Moore Mr. Roger Hernandez	Dear Messrs. Moore and Hernandez:
Married couple with same surname	Mr. and Mrs. Teles Archuleta	Dear Mr. and Mrs. Archuleta:
Married couple with different surnames	Ms. Sandra Cook Mr. Larry Strauss	Dear Ms. Cook and Mr. Strauss:
Attorney	Ms. Kathleen Bay, attorney-at-law *or* Kathleen Bay, Esq.	Dear Ms. Bay: *or* Dear Kathleen Bay, Esq.:
Physician	Hans Haydon, M.D. *or* Dr. Hans Haydon	Dear Dr. Haydon:
President of college or university	President James Riffee (name of university) *or* Dr. James Riffee President (name of university)	Dear President Riffee: *or* Dear Dr. Riffee:

When writing to a ...	Inside address	Salutation
Dean of college or university	Dean James Doluisio (name of school) (name of university) *or* Dr. James Doluisio Dean (name of school) (name of university)	Dear Dean Doluisio: or Dear Dr. Doluisio:
Professor of college or university	Professor Diane Ginsburg (name of department) (name of university) *or* Dr. (or Mr. or Ms.) Diane Ginsburg (name of department) (name of university)	Dear Professor Ginsburg: or Dear Dr. (or Mr. or Ms.) Ginsburg:
Superintendent of schools	Ms. (or Dr.) Kathleen Reilly Superintendent of (name of school district)	Dear Ms. (or Dr.) Reilly:
Principal	Mr. (or Ms.) Leslie Finn Principal (name of school) *or* Dr. Leslie Finn Principal (name of school)	Dear Mr. (or Ms.) Finn: or Dear Dr. Finn:
Teacher	Mr. (or Ms.) Pat Donaldson *or* Dr. Pat Donaldson (name of school)	Dear Mr. (or Ms.) Donaldson: *or* Dear Dr. Donaldson:

Postal abbreviations

States, territories, and possessions
When addressing letters and envelopes, follow the two-letter abbreviations authorized by the U.S. Postal Service. The recommended way to write abbreviations is to use capital letters with no periods or spaces between the letters.

Alabama	AL	Missouri	MO
Alaska	AK	Montana	MT
American Samoa	AS	Nebraska	NE
Arizona	AZ	Nevada	NV
Arkansas	AR	New Hampshire	NH
California	CA	New Jersey	NJ
Canal Zone	CZ	New Mexico	NM
Colorado	CO	New York	NY
Connecticut	CT	North Carolina	NC
Delaware	DE	North Dakota	ND
District of Columbia	DC	Ohio	OH
Florida	FL	Oklahoma	OK
Georgia	GA	Oregon	OR
Guam	GU	Pennsylvania	PA
Hawaii	HI	Puerto Rico	PR
Idaho	ID	Rhode Island	RI
Illinois	IL	South Carolina	SC
Indiana	IN	South Dakota	SD
Iowa	IA	Tennessee	TN
Kansas	KS	Texas	TX
Kentucky	KY	Utah	UT
Louisiana	LA	Vermont	VT
Maine	ME	Virginia	VA
Maryland	MD	Virgin Islands	VI
Massachusetts	MA	Washington	WA
Michigan	MI	West Virginia	WV
Minnesota	MN	Wisconsin	WI
Mississippi	MS	Wyoming	WY

Canadian provinces and territories

Alberta	AB	Nova Scotia	NS
British Columbia	BC	Ontario	ON
Labrador	LB	Prince Edward Island	PE
Manitoba	MB	Quebec	PQ
New Brunswick	NB	Saskatchewan	SK
Newfoundland	NF	Yukon	YT
Northwest Territories	NT		

RECOMMENDED RESOURCES

Tapes

Building a Dynamic Vocabulary. A. Rae Price. Boulder, Colo.: CareerTrack Publications, 1991 (audio).

Grammar for Business Professionals. Patricia Cramer. Boulder, Colo.: CareerTrack Publications, 1988 (audio), 1993 (video).

High-Impact Business Writing. Ronnie Moore. Boulder, Colo.: CareerTrack Publications, 1994 (audio/video).

How to Design Eye-Catching Brochures, Newsletters, Ads, Reports. Jane K. Cleland. Boulder, Colo.: CareerTrack Publications, 1995 (video).

How to Write a Winning Proposal. Patricia Cramer. Boulder, Colo.: CareerTrack Publications, 1995 (video).

Proofreading and Editing Skills. Debra Smith and Helen Sutton. Boulder, Colo.: CareerTrack Publications, 1992 (video).

Books

Business Letters for Busy People. Jim Dugger. Franklin Lakes, N.J.: Career Press, 1995.

Business Letter Writing. Sheryl Lindsell-Roberts. New York: Macmillan Inc., 1995.

The Gregg Reference Manual. William A. Sabin. Westerville, Ohio: Glencoe/McGraw-Hill, 1996.

Handbook for Practical Letter Writing. L. Sue Baugh. Lincolnwood, Ill.: NTC Business Books, 1995.

How to Create High-Impact Designs. Jane K. Cleland. Boulder, Colo.: CareerTrack Publications, 1995.

How to Create High-Impact Newsletters. Jane K. Cleland. Boulder, Colo.: CareerTrack Publications, 1996.

How to Say It. Rosalie Maggio. Englewood Cliffs, N.J.: Prentice Hall, 1990.

The New American Handbook of Letter Writing. Mary A. DeVries. New York: Penguin Books, 1988.

Powerful Proofreading Skills. Debra A. Smith and Helen R. Sutton. Menlo Park, Calif.: Crisp Publications Inc., 1994.

To the Letter. Dianna Booher. Lexington, Mass.: Lexington Books, 1988.